farmer's market
market
cookbook

farmer's market cookbook

Jacqueline Bellefontaine

© 2012 Kerswell Farm Ltd

This edition published by King Books

Printed 2012

This book is distributed in the UK by
Parkham Books Ltd
Barns Farm, Boraston
Tenbury Wells
Worcestershire
WR15 8NB

david@kingbooks.co.uk

ISBN: 978-1-906239-76-3

DS0260. farmer's market cookbook

Creative Director: Sarah King
Editor: Debbie Key
Designer: Debbie Fisher
Photographer: Colin Bowling/Paul Forrester

This material is a selection from *Farmer's Market - 100 Great Recipes*

Printed in Singapore

1 3 5 7 9 10 8 6 4 2

Contents

Introduction

I was delighted when I was asked to write a recipe book under the title of *Farmer's Market*. My favourite style of cooking – simple dishes using good-quality, seasonal produce – fitted the bill perfectly, and so this has been a most enjoyable book to write. You will not find long complicated recipes with numerous ingredients and complex cooking techniques. When you buy fresh produce, you should let the quality of the ingredients speak for themselves. A few of the recipes may have a long cooking time, but that doesn't mean you will be tied to the kitchen as you can just leave them to work their magic.

Variety is the spice of life and so you will discover that farmer's markets vary from place to place and from season to season. Every recipe in this book is based around one or more ingredients that can be bought from your local farmer's market, but because of the seasonality, you will not be able to make all of the recipes all of the time. Indeed, because farmer's markets sell local products and because this will vary around the country in some areas, you may not be able to get some of the items at all from your local farmer's market. All I ask is that you buy at least some of your ingredients from your farmer's market. Your reward is that you will then begin to discover the joy of buying good-quality, seasonal ingredients and the knock-on effects that this will have on your cooking. You will also discover that shopping for food can actually be fun!

What is a Farmer's Market?

A farmer's market is a market that sells foods from farmers, growers or producers, who come from a defined local area and sell direct to the public. All products sold should have been grown, reared, caught, brewed, pickled, baked, smoked or processed by the stallholder.

There will always be staples such as fruit and vegetables, salads, cheeses, meat, poultry, breads and eggs. But farmer's markets also sell speciality foodstuffs such as honey, juices, preserves, wine, cider, milk, cream, cakes, fish and herbs.

The produce is seasonal, so the stalls in a farmer's market will vary throughout the year, with the greatest choice in the summer and rather less in winter. However, you can expect to find unusual varieties and produce that you do not find in the supermarkets, such as quinces, sloes, golden beetroot, as well as unpasteurised milk and cream.

A true farmer's market will have no commercial stalls or stalls selling items that have not been produced locally.

Whilst farmer's markets promote high environmental and welfare standards, not all produce is organic. Nonetheless, a lot of organic producers do sell through farmer's markets, as they are an ideal outlet for those unable to produce the large quantities required by supermarkets. Farmer's markets are also often used as an outlet for farmers in the process of organic conversion, which is when a farmer is moving from conventional methods of farming to organic standards. This period can take a number of years, and by buying this produce you can help farmers through what can be a difficult time while they are undertaking more expensive farming techniques but are unable to charge the premium price that fully organic products command.

As the stall has to be manned by the suppliers and not by a third party, you are able to ask about production. The stallholders should be able to tell you the precise production history of everything they sell. This includes whether their vegetables are pesticide-free, or their eggs are organic. You can check how they control pests, how they house their pigs or what they feed their hens.

When did Farmer's Markets Start?

Back in history, all foods and goods were sold at markets, and these products were all locally produced. On the continent, food markets remained a part of the culture, but here in Britain, they all but disappeared and the food markets that remained were dominated by price rather than quality or regionality.

Farmer's markets, where the focus has returned to quality, freshness and the sale of locally produced foods, began in the USA. There, farmer's markets are now an established part of many local economies and have been flourishing for over 15 years.

The first modern-day farmer's market in Britain was held in Bath in September 1998. The first farmer's market in London was held almost a year later in Islington. Since these and other early fledgling markets, farmer's markets have quickly gone from strength to strength and there are now more than 500 farmer's markets in Britain. These are continuing to expand in numbers and size.

The popularity of farmer's markets is primarily due to the growing interest amongst consumers for fresh, locally produced foods and by farmers looking to supplement their income during what is a difficult time in farming.
Most farmer's markets are held on a specific day each month, others quarterly and some weekly. Some are also held more frequently during the summer months when there is the greatest amount of home produce available.

Why are Farmer's Markets Special?

The consumer benefits because:

- Farmer's markets provide direct contact and feedback between customers and producers, so you can find out more about how the food you eat is produced.
- They provide access to fresh, healthy produce.
- They offer value for money.
- They make shopping more enjoyable.
- You will find fruit and vegetable varieties and meat from animal breeds that are not available elsewhere.

The farmer/producer benefits because:

- The farmer/producer receives direct feedback from the consumer.
- Transport and packaging costs are reduced.
- Farmer's markets provide a secure regular market outlet.
- Farmer's markets cut out the middle man, increasing financial returns.

Farmer's markets benefit the environment because:

- They reduce food miles (the distance the food travels before it reaches the consumer).
- They reduce unnecessary packaging.
- They encourage environmentally friendly production practices, such as organic or pesticide-free.
- They encourage farming diversification and hence bio-diversity.

Farmer's markets benefit the community because:

- They help to bring new life to cities and towns and help regeneration.
- They stimulate local economies and keep money in the local community for longer, rather than money going straight to large companies.
- They attract extra business to local, established shopping areas.
- They reinforce local jobs and businesses

Why Shop at Farmer's Markets?

Surveys have shown that people support farmer's markets for a number of reasons:

- They want to support small farmers and producers.
- The food is freshly made or harvested.
- They can purchase organic produce.
- For the good-quality food.
- Out of curiosity because it makes a change from regular shopping.
- For the friendlier, relaxed atmosphere.

These same surveys also indicated that most people's main reason for shopping at supermarkets is convenience. It was felt that farmer's markets offer more of what people actually want, and that there should be more of them to make them more convenient.

Whilst shopping at supermarkets certainly offers a convenient one-stop shop for the weekly food, supermarkets can seldom be described as friendly and fun. Farmer's markets are usually bustling and are on a more human scale. True, shopping at farmer's markets will take longer and you will probably still have to go to the supermarket, but you can ask advice, not only about how the food was produced, but also the best way to cook it. In the USA, where farmer's markets have been established for many years, farmers have modified their farming practices to suit local consumers. This proves that you have every chance to tell the farmers what you want, and that they will respond to this feedback.

value for Money

An expectation by consumers for increasingly cheaper food means that for markets to survive, the consumer must be prepared to source quality food and be prepared to pay a bit extra for it in comparison to prices in the supermarkets. Supermarket prices are based on high volumes of production, the very opposite of typical farmer's market stallholders. However, this doesn't necessarily mean that shopping from farmer's markets comes out very expensive overall. As you can only buy food that is in season, you will not be paying over the odds for food to be produced out of season and transported hundreds, or even thousands of miles.

One of the benefits of farmer's markets is that they enable the farmer to cut out the 'middle man'. Farmers often have little choice about accepting low prices for some items from supermarkets, yet this is not usually reflected in the sale price. Through farmer's markets, it may be possible for a farmer to increase profits, yet still be cheaper than a conventional store. UK evidence so far finds that farmer's market prices are competitive and that organic foods at farmer's markets are often cheaper. Nonetheless, because many farmer's markets stock food produced less intensively, production costs will be higher. Hopefully, this is reflected by higher quality goods, albeit in terms of flavour, animal welfare, or reduction in chemicals or pesticides used. As consumers, we must be prepared to pay extra for quality. Farmer's markets may not be the cheapest place for food shopping, but when comparing like-for-like, they offer excellent value for money.

Choice

One of the great things about shopping at a farmer's market is the variety of choice. The nature of farmer's markets makes them ideal outlets for specialist local produce such as unusual fruit and vegetable varieties, wild boar sausages, rare breed meats or buffalo cheeses. You will find food at farmer's markets that you cannot get in supermarkets. For example, quinces are not produced in commercially viable quantities for supermarkets, yet a farmer can bring just one box to sell at market. Three varieties of pears account for 94% of pears grown commercially in the UK and yet there are over 550 varieties of eating and cooking pears in the national fruit collection at Brogdale in Kent. When the farmer does not have to supply the large quantities that supermarkets require, they can grow and sell more varieties. So, in some areas you will find many more varieties of fruit and vegetables available than you could possibly find in the shops.

Why are Farmer's Markets Good for Farmers?

The future of farming in the UK is increasingly reliant on selling produce based on quality and reputation and by making stronger links with communities. Farmer's markets are an excellent way to allow otherwise struggling farmers to keep their heads above water. They can provide a vital survival route for small-scale producers, providing extra and alternative sources of income.

Several farmers in the UK have said that they would be out of business if it wasn't for their local farmer's market. This has also proved to be the case in the USA, where out of 20,000 farmers surveyed, 37% said they would have gone out of business without a local farmer's market.

Small-scale farmers do not have to worry about producing the large quantities required by supermarkets, nor the specifications for size, shape, or appearance dictated by them. Neither do they have to worry about consumers, as they now have an additional market to sell their produce.

What are the Benefits to the Environment?

There is a slow change in emphasis towards more sustainable farming. For farmers making this transition, farmer's markets are often ideal places to sell their produce.

Currently, food can travel hundreds of miles – known as 'food miles – before it reaches our homes. This is true even if the food is grown in the UK. Take for example a potato bought from your local supermarket. Although it may have been grown close to your home it may travel a hundred miles to a packaging plant. Then, it may be taken more miles to a supermarket distribution centre and then even more miles to your local supermarket. Farmer's markets cut these food miles to a minimum, giving two advantages. First, the food is fresher when it reaches its point of sale. Secondly, it benefits the environment by saving the fuel needed to transport the food on its epic journey, and by reducing the amount of packaging needed to protect the food. It may even have the added bonus of being cheaper, as the cost of transport and packaging is negligible.

If, as consumers, we can make the move away from expecting foods to be available all year round, maybe we can reduce our reliance on imported foods from around the globe. If we managed this most of the time, this would significantly reduce the environmental costs of transporting these foods. Every farmer's market regulation stipulates that only locally grown produce is sold, so you can be confident that what you buy is in season. It is neither practical nor desirable to have all our foods produced locally, but by buying seasonally and locally when we can, we are doing our small bit to help the environment.

What are the Benefits to the Local Community?

Farmer's markets benefit the local economy, as they encourage agricultural diversification and attract people to local businesses. Research by the National Farmers' Union shows that 80% of neighbouring businesses have seen a boost in trade following the establishment of a market nearby. Even supermarkets can see an increase in trade on market days.

Farmer's markets encourage small-scale, less intensive production, provide a social meeting point and encourage goodwill and understanding.

There is a need for greater co-operation between local producers and local consumers and the connections of countryside to local towns and cities need to be re-established.

Farmer's markets help to keep money in the local economy for longer, rather than going straight to large firms and organisations.

The National Farmers' Retail and Markets Association

In order for farmer's markets to continue to grow in numbers, it is essential that they are supported by consumers. This requires a change in our shopping habits, away from one-stop shopping. We have to accept that choice will be more restricted in that we will have to start to shop seasonally, but we will be rewarded with greater choices of varieties when in season.

As consumers, we need the reassurance that the food we buy at farmer's markets really is locally produced and of a good quality, enabling us to feel truly confident in what we buy from these markets.

Around half the farmer's markets currently established in the UK are members of the National Farmers' Retail & Markets Association (FARMA). FARMA was set up to establish a set of criteria for the markets to adhere to, in order to maintain their integrity. Membership is voluntary. In June 2002, certification was launched to independently verify market standards and reward genuine farmer's markets with a distinctive logo.

Whilst very good farmer's markets exist that are not members of FARMA, certification of farmer's markets is an important step forward in that it provides the reassurance required by consumers. If your farmer's market is a member, you can be sure it is the genuine thing.

As a general guide, Members of the National Farmers' Retail & Markets Association should:

- Only sell foods that are produced locally within a defined area. Local usually means within a 30-mile radius, although up to 50 miles is acceptable for larger cities and coastal or remote towns and villages. Alternatively, there may be a boundary, e.g. a county or other geographical boundary such as a National Park, that defines the local area. It is recommended that no produce should come from more than 100 miles of the market. (All London farmer's market stallholders come from within 100 miles of the M25, many are nearer.)

- The principal producer, or a representative directly involved in the production process, must attend the stall. This allows consumers to ask about all aspects of the production of the food. It is a key principle that farmer's markets allow the consumer to have a direct relationship with the producer.

- All produce sold must be grown, reared and caught by the stallholder within the defined local area. For livestock and plants, this means grown or finished on the producer's land. Livestock must have spent at least 50% of its life on that land. Game can be shot or caught in the defined area by a person licensed to hunt game. Fish should be sold by the fisherman, or by a representative of a number of boats so long as the fishing grounds are local inshore water.

- Processed foods must be brewed, pickled, baked, smoked or processed by the stallholder using at least one ingredient of origin from the defined local area. Local ingredients must account for at least 10% of the produce.

- All markets should have available for their customers information about the rules of the market and the production methods of the producers.

About this Book

Farmer's markets promote a more sustainable society, reducing food miles and assisting in the sale and marketing of food produced to high environmental and welfare standards.

Following the ethos of farmer's markets and caring about where my food comes from, I always buy free-range eggs and chicken. I like to use unrefined sugars and use organic produce wherever possible. I also buy Fair Trade goods such as coffee, bananas etc. Fair Trade ensures that farmers in other parts of the world get a fair price for their produce.

I have broken the book down into five chapters:

- Meat, poultry, fish and game
- Vegetables
- Cheese and dairy
- Fruits
- Snacks and treats

These chapters represent the main groups of produce available from farmer's markets. Inevitably, there are some overlaps, with recipes that could go into more than one chapter. Whether you choose to make a recipe and go and buy the produce from the market, or better still, see what is best value at the market that week, bring it home and then see what you can make with your bounty, I hope you will find that this book works for you and that you will soon be enjoying the farmer's market way of shopping and cooking.

Meat, Poultry, Fish and Game

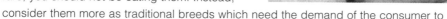

When purchasing meat, ask about the breed and animal welfare. Where possible, buy native breeds. If you are lucky enough to have suppliers of rare breeds, do not be put off by the term and feel that because they are rare, you should not be eating them. Instead, consider them more as traditional breeds which need the demand of the consumer to

ensure their survival. Just as different varieties of fruit taste different, so different breeds of animals have their own unique characteristics and flavours. Many of the rare-breed meats became rare because they did not suit modern, more intensive methods of production, as they mature more slowly and usually on a natural diet. As a result, their meat is of a higher quality. I urge you to try these traditional breeds. In doing so, you are ensuring their survival and will be in for a truly great taste experience.

After buying meat, remove the wrapping and dry if necessary. Keep loosely covered in the refrigerator. Fresh meat will keep in the refrigerator for two to three days. Minced meat and offal is best used on the day of purchase.

Cheese and Dairy

As farmer's markets only stock local produce, the cheeses that you purchase from them will vary from region to region. Therefore, in the recipes in this section of the book I have generally suggested a type of cheese, e.g. hard, soft, or blue cheese, rather than a specific cheese. This means that there will be variations in the flavour of the dishes, depending on what part of the country you live in and what cheeses are available. This, I think, is one of the pleasures of shopping and cooking with farmer's market produce – the recipes will not be universally the same.

There are more than 400 different cheeses produced in Britain, so enjoy experimenting with the cheeses available. If in doubt regarding their suitability, ask the stallholder. Hard cheeses such as Cheddar, Double Gloucester, Cheshire and Red Leicester are firmly pressed during processing. Semi-hard cheeses such as Lancashire and Caerphilly, are only lightly pressed and have a crumbly texture. Soft cheeses such as Crowdie, curd and cream cheese are not pressed at all, but are allowed to drain. Blue cheeses such as Stilton are injected with moulds to give a blue veining.

To test the recipes for this book, I tried to use as many different cheeses as possible all purchased from farmer's markets.

At farmer's markets, you may be able to purchase unpasteurised milk which can only be bought direct from the farmer.

Vegetables and Fruit

Freshness is all-important when buying fruits and vegetables and here, farmer's markets come into their own. Because the produce is grown locally, it has far less distance to travel before reaching you. It can be on the stall for sale within a matter of hours, rather than days, after being harvested.

Buying Vegetables:

Root vegetables
- Avoid too much dirt on vegetables, but do expect them to be dirty. Supermarket vegetables are always cleaned.
- Make sure the vegetables are firm and not shrivelled.
- Avoid large swedes that may have woody centres.
- If buying bunched carrots, the tops should look fresh.

Green vegetables
- Choose vegetables with a bright and strong colour.
- Avoid those with yellow-tinged leaves.
- Store wrapped in paper bags or newspaper.

Salad vegetables
- Select fresh looking leaves.
- Cucumbers should be firm.
- Salad onions should have fresh unshrivelled leaves.

Buying Fruit:

Apples and pears
- Avoid fruit with bruises

Summer fruit
- Avoid very soft fruits with any signs of mushiness.
- Choose strawberries with good all-over colour, avoiding those with unripened white flesh around the stem.

What's in Season?

Some products at farmer's markets are not available all year round, especially fruit and vegetables. However, farmers are putting up more polytunnels and hothouses each year, thereby extending the seasons of many of our fruits and vegetables. Nevertheless, the farmer still has to rely on sun and rain, so supply will vary. Although this is not an exhaustive list, it will give you an idea as to what's in season and when.

Spring	Summer	Autumn	Winter
Asparagus	Beetroot	Celery	Bay leaves
Beetroot	Broad beans	Chestnuts	Beetroot
Carrots	Carrots	Cobnuts	Brussels sprouts
Cauliflower	Cauliflower	Damsons	Cabbage
Celeriac	Celery	Elderberries	Carrots
Cucumbers	Courgettes	Mushrooms	Cauliflower
Curly kale	Cucumbers	Hazelnuts	Celery
New potatoes	Fennel	Leeks	Celeriac
Mint	Peas	Lettuce	Chard
Parsley	Pea shoots	Marrow	Chestnuts
Purple-sprouting broccoli	Garlic	Pumpkin	Curly kale
Rosemary	Globe artichokes	Rocket	Jerusalem artichokes
Savoy cabbage	Green beans	Sweetcorn	Leeks
Spinach	Lettuce and salad leaves	Watercress	Red cabbages
Spring onions	New potatoes		Swedes
Watercress	Sage	Apples	Turnips
Rhubarb	Sweetcorn	Blackberries	Parsnips
	Tomatoes	Pears	Walnuts
	Watercress	Plums	
Crab		Sloes	Apples
Haddock	Cherries	Quince	Pears
Lobster	Gooseberries		
Mackerel	Greengages	Brill	Mussels
Sea bass	Plums	Dover sole	Oysters
Salmon	Raspberries	Oysters	
	Red and black currants		Partridge
Single Gloucester	Strawberries	Double Gloucester	Pheasant
cheeses		cheese	Wild duck
Soft cheeses	Crab		Hare
	Pilchard	Grouse	
Duck and goose eggs	Wild salmon		
Spring lamb			
Pigeon			

Snacks and Treats

Most farmer's markets have at least one or two stalls of locally produced, processed foods and drinks such as jams, preserves, condiments, juices, cordials, breads, cakes and pies.

Jams and preserves bought from farmer's markets can be the next best thing to home-made. Breads and cakes are made on a smaller scale by traditional methods. The results are much different from other commercially produced breads and cakes and, again, well worth a try.

Some markets also stock products such as honey and mustard which are ideal for use in home cooking. Some honeys may have strong flavours which can dominate the taste of a dish. Taste first and if in doubt, ask advice.

Nowhere else will you find such a mixture of fresh, locally produced goods, than at a farmer's market. What could be better than good-quality, traceable, fresh seasonal and local foods?

I hope you enjoy shopping from farmer's markets and cooking from this book as much as I have enjoyed researching and writing it. However, one thing is certain, people who care about what they eat, about how food is produced and the impact on the environment can take a step in the right direction to improve things for the better by using local farmer's markets, and getting to know their suppliers.

Happy shopping!

Tips for Successful Cooking

- Use metric or imperial measurements only; do not mix the two.

- Use measuring spoons: 1 tsp = 5ml; 1 tbsp = 15ml

- All spoon measurements are level unless otherwise stated.

- All eggs are medium unless otherwise stated.

- Recipes using raw or lightly cooked eggs should not be given to babies, pregnant women, the very old or anyone suffering from or recovering from an illness.

- The cooking times are an approximate guide only. If you are using a fan-oven reduce the cooking time according to the manufacturer's instructions.

- Ovens should be preheated to the required temperature.

- Fruits and vegetables should be washed before use.

Finding your nearest farmer's market:

For a complete list of farmer's markets registered with the National Farmers' Retail & Markets Association, log on to www.farma.org.uk or call 0845 4588420.

meat,
poultry,
fish
and game

Pot Roast Brisket

Family Favourite

This recipe is a great meal to make after a trip to the farmer's market, for both the meat and vegetables. I like brisket as it is an economical joint for this dish, but if your stall doesn't have brisket, ask the stallholder what other meat they would recommend. It is a good chance to make friends with your supplier. I often make this into two meals, serving the meat hot with the vegetables and gravy on day one, and then cold the following day accompanied by chips and tomatoes, or jacket potatoes and beans.

Ingredients for 8

1.3kg/3lb rolled brisket
225g/8oz shallots or small onions
700g/1½lb mixed root vegetables, such as carrots, parsnips,
   swede and turnips
25g/1oz beef dripping or 2 tbsp sunflower oil
300ml/½ pint beef stock
Few sprigs fresh thyme
2 bay leaves
175g/6oz button mushrooms (optional)
Salt and freshly ground black pepper

1 Preheat the oven to 170°C/325°F/Gas mark 3. Season the brisket. If using onions, cut into quarters. Peel and cut the root vegetables into large chunks.

2 Heat the dripping or oil in a large flameproof casserole and brown the meat on all sides. You may find it easier to brown the meat in a frying pan and transfer it to a casserole dish.

3 Add the root vegetables, stock, thyme and bay leaf. Cover and cook for 2 hours.

4 Add the mushrooms (if using) and return to the oven for another 30 minutes.

5 Slice the meat and surround with vegetables. Spoon gravy over, or serve separately.

Steak & Kidney Pudding

This is filling and warming, making it perfect for winter days.

Ingredients for 2

350g/12oz stewing steak, cut
  into 2.5cm/1 inch cubes
100g/4oz ox kidney, cored
  and cut into cubes
2 tsp plain flour
1 tsp dried mixed herbs
About 1 tbsp sunflower oil
1 small onion, chopped
75ml/2½fl oz red wine
75g/3oz chestnut
  mushrooms, quartered
  or sliced
150ml/¼ pint beef stock
Salt and freshly ground
  black pepper

Suet Pastry:

175g/6oz self-raising flour
75g/3oz vegetable or beef
  suet
1 tbsp fresh parsley, chopped
1 small free-range egg yolk
Cold water to mix

Ingredients for 4

700g/1½lb stewing steak, cut
  into 2.5cm/1 inch cubes
175g/6oz ox kidney, cored
  and cut into cubes
4 tsp plain flour
2 tsp dried mixed herbs
About 2 tbsp sunflower oil
1 onion, chopped
150ml/¼ pint red wine
225g/8oz chestnut
  mushrooms, quartered
  or sliced
300ml/½ pint beef stock
Salt and freshly ground
  black pepper

Suet Pastry:

300g/10½oz self-raising flour
150g/5oz vegetable or beef
  suet
2 tbsp fresh parsley, chopped
1 free-range egg yolk
Cold water to mix

1 Place the meat and kidney in a plastic bag, add the flour and herbs, season with salt and pepper and shake well.

2 Heat half the oil in a large frying pan and fry the onions until golden brown and softened. Transfer to a saucepan.

3 Add the remaining oil and floured meat, brown on all sides using a little extra oil if required. Add to the saucepan.

4 Bring the red wine to the boil in the frying pan. Pour over the meat. Put the mushrooms and stock in the saucepan and bring to the boil. Reduce the heat, cover and simmer for 1 hour.

5 To make the pastry, place the flour in a bowl and stir in the suet and parsley. Season with salt and pepper.

6 Make a well in the centre and add the egg yolk. Add enough water to mix to a soft dough.

7 Using just over two thirds of the pastry roll out to form a circle and use to line a greased 600ml/1 pint (1.2 litres/2 pint) heatproof basin.

8 Spoon the meat mixture into the lined basin. Roll out the remaining pastry and use to make a lid for the pudding. Dampen the edges of the pastry to seal.

9 Cover loosely with greaseproof paper and foil. Place in a large saucepan and fill with boiling water to come two-thirds of the way up the basin. Cover and simmer gently for 1 hour (1½ hours). Keep an eye on the water level and top up if required.

10 Carefully remove the bowl from the water and turn out the pudding on to a plate to serve or serve straight from the bowl.

Old-fashioned Beef Stew with Parsley Dumplings

Family Favourite

A perfect meal for cold winter days. You can cook the stew ahead of time, then reheat and add the dumplings when required. Once you add the dumplings you can cover the stew, in which case, the dumplings will steam and remain soft all over. Alternatively, you can leave the stew uncovered and the dumplings will bake, resulting in a golden crispy top.

Ingredients for 2

450g/1lb braising or chuck steak, cut into cubes
1 tbsp plain flour
About 1 tbsp sunflower oil
1 onion, sliced
450ml/¾ pint beef stock
350g/12oz mixed root vegetables such as carrots, turnips, potatoes and parsnips, cut into chunks
Few sprigs thyme
1 bay leaf

Dumplings:

75g/3oz self-raising flour
40g/1½oz suet
2 tbsp fresh parsley, chopped
About 2–3 tbsp milk
Salt and freshly ground black pepper

Ingredients for 4

900g/2lb braising or chuck steak, cut into cubes
2 tbsp plain flour
About 2 tbsp sunflower oil
2 onions, sliced
900ml/1½ pint beef stock
700g/1½lb mixed root vegetables such as carrots, turnips, potatoes and parsnips, cut into chunks
Few sprigs thyme
2 bay leaves

Dumplings:

175g/6oz self-raising flour
75g/3oz suet
4 tbsp fresh parsley, chopped
About 4–5 tbsp milk
Salt and freshly ground black pepper

1 Preheat the oven to 180°C/350°F/Gas mark 4.

2 Place the meat in a plastic bag, add the flour and some salt and pepper and shake well.

3 Heat the oil in a frying pan and fry the onion for 3 minutes until softened. Transfer to a large ovenproof casserole.

4 Add the meat to the pan and cook over a high heat until browned on all sides, adding a little extra oil if required.

5 Stir in the stock and bring to the boil. Pour into the casserole dish. Stir in the vegetables, thyme and bay leaves. Cover and cook for 1½–2 hours, or until meat is very tender.

6 To make the dumplings, place the flour in a bowl and stir in the suet and parsley. Season lightly. Add enough milk to mix to a soft dough. Roll into 8 balls.

7 Remove the lid from the casserole and arrange the dumplings on top. Cook covered or uncovered for a further 30 minutes.

Oven-roast Venison with Mustard Cream

Quick and Easy

Venison is a very lean meat, so I like to serve it with a sauce. It is quite a rich meat, so a little goes a long way.

Ingredients 3-4

300g/10½oz venison haunch
1 tsp beef dripping or
    olive oil
1 tbsp thick honey
1 tbsp dry sherry or brandy
4 tbsp double cream
1 tsp whole grain mustard
Salt and freshly ground
    black pepper

Ingredients for 6-8

600g/1lb 5oz venison haunch
1 tbsp beef dripping or
    olive oil
2 tbsp thick honey
2 tbsp dry sherry or brandy
100ml/3½fl oz double cream
2 tsp whole grain mustard
Salt and freshly ground
    black pepper

1 Preheat the oven to 200°C/400°F/Gas mark 6.

2 Heat the dripping or oil in a frying pan and fry the meat quickly on all sides to brown. Transfer to a roasting tin and roast for 15–20 minutes (35–40 minutes).

3 When the meat is cooked, transfer to a warm plate and keep warm. Stir the honey and sherry or brandy into the hot roasting tin, then stir in the cream and mustard.

4 Cook over a low heat until the sauce begins to boil, continue to cook, stirring until the sauce is reduced and thickened a little.

5 Carve the meat and serve with the sauce poured over.

Lamb Shanks glazed with Apple Juice

Ideally, use a single variety apple juice with a dry flavour such as Bramley apple.

Ingredients for 2

2 lamb shanks
1 tbsp sunflower oil
1 onion, cut into wedges
1 clove garlic, sliced
Grated zest and juice of ½
    unwaxed lemon
150ml/¼ pint English apple
    juice
150ml/¼ pint white wine
Salt and freshly ground
    black pepper
Cornflour (optional)

Ingredients for 4

4 lamb shanks
2 tbsp sunflower oil
2 onions, cut into wedges
2 cloves garlic, sliced
Grated zest and juice of 1
    unwaxed lemon
300ml/½ pint English apple
    juice
300ml/½ pint white wine
Salt and freshly ground
    black pepper
Cornflour (optional)

1 Preheat the oven to 180°C/350°F/Gas mark 4. Season the lamb shanks.

2 Heat the oil in a large frying pan and fry the shanks until browned on all sides. Transfer the lamb shanks to a large, ovenproof dish.

3 Add the onions to the pan and sauté gently for 4–5 minutes, until just golden.

4 Stir in the garlic and cook for 1 minute. Stir in the lemon zest, lemon juice, apple juice and wine. Bring to the boil.

5 Pour over the lamb. Cover and cook in the oven for 2–2½ hours until the meat is very tender, basting occasionally.

6 Transfer the lamb and onions to warm serving plates. Spoon off any fat from the cooking liquor. Thicken with a little cornflour if desired. Taste and adjust the seasoning if required. Serve the sauce poured over the lamb shanks.

Roast Pork

Family Favourite

I find, generally, that the larger the joint, the better it cooks. So I have not reduced the quantities for this recipe. It is far better to cook a larger joint and serve the rest cold the following day. A favourite of mine is to serve cold meat with chips, but a jacket potato is a healthier option and is just as convenient. You may be lucky enough to have a supplier of rare breed pork, such as Gloucester Old Spot. If so, take advantage as the flavour is divine.

Ingredients for 6–8

Boneless shoulder or leg pork joint, e.g. Gloucester old spot, about 1.3–1.5kg/3 to 3¼lb in weight
Salt
1 tbsp plain flour
300ml/½ pint chicken or vegetable stock.

1 When you get the meat home, unwrap the joint and place uncovered on a plate until required. This allows the skin to dry and improves the crackling. If you are cooking immediately, dab the joint dry with kitchen paper.

2 Preheat the oven to 220°C/425°F/Gas mark 7. Weigh the joint and calculate the cooking time. Allow 25 minutes per 500g, plus 25 minutes.

3 Place the meat in a roasting tin and sprinkle the skin with sea salt. Roast for 45 minutes, then reduce the oven temperature to 180°C/350°F/Gas mark 4 for the remaining cooking time, basting once or twice during cooking. When cooked, the juices should run clear when pierced with a skewer.

4 Allow to rest for 15 minutes before carving. To make carving easier, remove the crackling first and then carve the joint.

5 To make the gravy, stir the flour into the roasting tin and cook for a few seconds over a low heat. Stir in the stock and cook, stirring until the gravy thickens.

Baked, Honey-glazed Gammon

One Pot

Home-cooked ham tastes far better than any you can buy ready-sliced in the shops. It's ideal for picnics, celebrations or even midweek meals, and can be served hot or cold – making it a truly versatile meat. It can be stored in the refrigerator for up to one week.

Ingredients for 8–12

Gammon joint about 1.5kg/3lb 6oz
Whole cloves
4–6 tbsp local honey

1 Preheat the oven to 180°C/350°F/Gas mark 4.

2 Line a roasting tin with a piece of foil that is large enough to wrap the joint. Place the gammon in a roasting tin on the foil and gather up the foil to enclose the joint. Calculate the cooking time and roast for 25 minutes per 500g/1lb 2oz, plus 25 minutes.

3 Half an hour before the end of the cooking time, remove the gammon from the oven, and carefully cut away the rind, leaving as much fat as possible.

4 Cut a crisscross pattern over the joint with a small, sharp knife and push a clove into the fat where each line crosses.

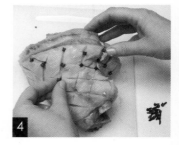

5 Warm the honey gently in a small pan and brush liberally all over the joint. Return to the roasting tin, placing back on the foil, but this time do not cover the joint with the foil. Return to the oven and bake uncovered for the remaining 30 minutes until the rind is golden.

6 If serving hot, allow to stand for 15 minutes before carving.

Toad in the Hole

Family Favourite

A favourite recipe from my childhood – my mum made the best toad in the hole and Yorkshire puddings without measuring the ingredients. Unfortunately, I don't inherit these talents, but I do find that this batter recipe works well. It's no good using run-of-the-mill sausages for this recipe, only good sausages will do.

Ingredients for 2

100g/4oz plain flour
Pinch salt
1 large free-range egg
300ml/½ pint milk
1 tsp sunflower oil.
4 good pork sausages

Ingredients for 4

200g/7oz plain flour
Pinch salt
2 large free-range eggs
500ml/18fl oz milk
2 tsp sunflower oil
8 good pork sausages

1 Preheat the oven to 220°C/425°F/Gas mark 7.

2 Place the flour, salt, egg and milk in a food processor or liquidizer and blend well. Allow to stand for 10 minutes.

3 Pour the oil into a 18cm/7 inch square cake tin (23cm/9 inch cake tin or medium roasting tin) and swirl to coat the base and sides. Make sure it is not a loose-based cake tin or the batter will run out.

4 Place the sausages in the tin. Bake in the oven for 5 minutes.

5 Pour the batter over the hot sausages and return to the oven and bake for 20 minutes, then reduce the heat to 190°C/375°F/Gas mark 5 and bake for a further 30–45 minutes until the batter is risen, crisp and golden.

6 Serve at once with lashings of gravy.

Pot-roast Chicken

Family Favourite

Pot roasting gives a really succulent roast chicken.

Ingredients for 4–6

1.5kg/3lb free-range chicken
3 tbsp sunflower oil
2 onions, cut into wedges
900g/2lb new potatoes
450ml/¾ pint chicken or vegetable stock
2 tsp cornflour mixed with a little water (optional)
Salt and freshly ground black pepper
Pinch freshly grated nutmeg

1 Preheat the oven to 190°C/375°F/Gas mark 5. Season the chicken with salt pepper and a pinch of nutmeg.

2 Heat 2 tablespoons of the oil in a large frying pan and brown the chicken on all sides. Transfer to a large ovenproof casserole.

3 Arrange the onions and potatoes around the chicken.

4 Cover and place in the centre of the oven for 1½ hours until the chicken is tender and the juices run clear.

5 Transfer the chicken to a serving plate and keep warm. Remove the vegetables with a draining spoon and keep warm.

6 Spoon any fat from the stock in the pan and thicken with a little cornflour if preferred, or serve as a thin gravy.

7 Serve the chicken with the vegetables and the gravy.

Chicken Liver Pâté with Sage & Shallots

Quick and Easy

Chicken livers can be hard to find in the supermarket these days, yet I have seen them at many of the farmer's markets I have visited. They are delicious pan-fried, then sprinkled with a little balsamic vinegar, or a splash of sherry and served on toast. But here, I have made them into a simple pâté, great for sandwiches, spreading on toast or some of the fantastic breads that you can buy from the markets.

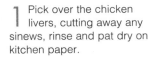

Ingredients for 2

150g/5oz chicken livers
75g/3oz butter
1 shallot, finely chopped
1 clove garlic, chopped
1 tsp brandy or sherry
1 tsp fresh sage, chopped
or ¼ tsp dried sage

Ingredients for 4

250g/9oz chicken livers
175g/6oz butter
2 shallots, finely chopped
2 cloves garlic, chopped
1 tbsp brandy or sherry
1 tbsp fresh sage, chopped
or 1½ tsp dried sage

1 Pick over the chicken livers, cutting away any sinews, rinse and pat dry on kitchen paper.

2 Melt about one-quarter of the butter in a frying pan and sauté the shallots for 2 minutes, until just softened. Add the chicken livers and garlic and fry over a medium heat for about 5 minutes until the chicken livers are cooked through.

3 Stir in the brandy or sherry, sage and half the remaining butter. Stir until the butter has melted. Transfer to a food processor, season and blend until smooth. Transfer to large, or individual, serving pots. Level the top.

4 Gently melt the remaining butter in a small pan without stirring. Remove from the heat and allow to stand for a few minutes. Pour off the butter fat and discard the white sediment at the bottom of the pan. This is known as clarifying the butter.

5 Pour a little clarified butter over the pate and chill until required.

Marmalade Duck

Duck has a rich, meaty flavour. In autumn you may be lucky enough to find wild duck which has an even greater depth of flavour. It works well with orange, and here a simple glacé of marmalade is used. Some farmer's markets have stalls that sell home-made or small-scale production preserves. So try to pick up some marmalade from the market.

Ingredients for 2

- **2 duck leg portions**
- **2 tbsp thin-shred marmalade**
- **1 tsp root ginger, grated (optional)**
- **1 tbsp lemon juice**
- **1 tsp soy sauce**
- **½ tsp wholegrain mustard**

Ingredients for 4

- **4 duck leg portions**
- **4 tbsp thin-shred marmalade**
- **2 tsp root ginger, grated (optional)**
- **2 tbsp lemon juice**
- **2 tsp soy sauce**
- **1 tsp wholegrain mustard**

1 Preheat the oven to 180°C/350°F/Gas mark 4.

2 Prick the duck legs all over with a fork.

3 Combine the marmalade, ginger (if using), lemon juice, soy and mustard together in a small bowl.

4 Brush liberally over the duck legs.

5 Place in a shallow, roasting tin and roast for 45 minutes until the duck is crisp and golden. Brush any remaining glaze over the legs once or twice as it cooks.

Sole with Watercress Sauce

Easy Entertaining

Dover sole is an expensive fish, but its flavour is so delicious, it is worth the occasional treat. Lemon sole can be substituted, but the flavour is quite different. In fact, the sauce will go with any white fish as well as salmon, so you can ring the changes according to what is available at the market.

Ingredients for 2

- ½ bunch watercress
- 2 Dover or lemon sole, cleaned
- 15g/½oz butter
- 1 tbsp sunflower oil
- 75ml/2½fl oz dry white wine
- 75ml/2½fl oz double cream
- ¼ tsp cornflour
- Salt and freshly ground black pepper

Ingredients for 4

- 1 bunch watercress
- 4 Dover or lemon sole, cleaned
- 25g/1oz butter
- 2 tbsp sunflower oil
- 150ml/¼ pint dry white wine
- 150ml/¼ pint double cream
- ½ tsp cornflour
- Salt and freshly ground black pepper

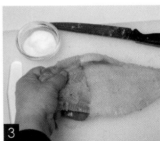

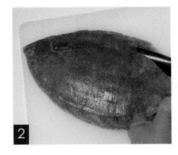

1 Wash the watercress and shake dry. Discard any tough stalks (small tender stalks are fine), and chop finely.

2 Season the fish. Cut the skirt from the edge of the fish with sharp scissors.

3 You can skin the fish before cooking, if desired. Cut a little slash into the skin at the tail end of the fish and use a sawing motion to cut a little of the skin away from the flesh. Once you have enough skin to get hold of, dip your fingers in salt to make gripping the fish easier and carefully pull away the skin. If you are unsure about doing this, the fish can be left with the skin on, simply cut a couple of slashes into the fish before cooking.

4 Melt the butter and oil in a large frying pan and pan-fry the fish for 3-5 minutes each side. You may need to do this in two batches. Remove from the pan to a warm plate, cover loosely with foil and keep warm.

5 Add the wine to the pan and increase the heat. Boil until you have about 1–2 (2–3) tablespoons left.

6 Mix a little of the cream with the cornflour, then stir into the rest of the cream. Add to the pan and cook, stirring, until thickened slightly. Stir in the watercress and cook for a moment or two longer to heat through.

7 Serve the fish with the sauce poured over.

Roast Pheasant with Apple and Cider

Easy to prepare, this dish is full of flavour. Remember, the bird may contain traces of lead shot, which should be cut away and discarded.

Ingredients for 2

- 1 oven-ready pheasant
- 1 lemon wedge
- 25g/1oz butter
- 2 rashers streaky bacon from outdoor-reared pigs
- 1 eating apple
- 3 tbsp dry cider
- ½ tsp wholegrain mustard
- 2 tbsp chicken stock
- 2 tbsp double cream

Ingredients for 4

- 2 oven-ready pheasants
- 2 lemon wedges
- 50g/2oz butter
- 4 rashers streaky bacon from outdoor-reared pigs
- 2 eating apples
- 90ml/3fl oz dry cider
- 1 tsp wholegrain mustard
- 50ml/2fl oz chicken stock
- 75ml/2½fl oz double cream

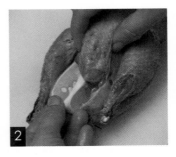

1 Preheat the oven to 200°C/400°F/Gas mark 6. Rinse each bird inside and out and pat dry with kitchen paper.

2 Place a wedge of lemon and a knob of butter into the body cavity of each bird.

3 Place in a roasting tin. Dot the remaining butter over the birds and lay the bacon over the breast of each pheasant.

4 Roast for about 20 minutes and baste with the juices.

5 Core and quarter the apples and arrange in the pan around the birds and continue to roast for 25–30 minutes or until the juices run clear.

6 Transfer the pheasants and apple quarters to a warm serving plate.

7 Place the roasting tin over a medium heat and add the cider, stirring to incorporate the pan juices. Add the mustard, stock and cream and bring to the boil.

8 Boil rapidly, stirring until the sauce thickens slightly.

9 Season with salt and pepper and serve the sauce with the pheasant.

Pigeon Braised in Red Wine

Pigeon is best suited to a slow cooking method to ensure that the end result is not tough.

Ingredients for 2

- 1 tbsp olive oil
- 2 pigeons, halved
- 1 small onion, sliced
- 1 clove garlic, chopped
- 1 tsp juniper berries, lightly crushed
- 1 tsp plain flour
- 150ml/¼ pint red wine
- 100g/4oz chestnut mushrooms, quartered
- 1 tbsp redcurrant jelly or cranberry sauce

Ingredients for 4

- 2 tbsp olive oil
- 4 pigeons, halved
- 1 large onion, sliced
- 2 cloves garlic, chopped
- 2 tsp juniper berries, lightly crushed
- 2 tsp plain flour
- 300ml/½ pint red wine
- 225g/8oz chestnut mushrooms, quartered
- 2 tbsp redcurrant jelly or cranberry sauce

1 Heat oil in a large frying pan and brown the pigeon. Transfer to a flameproof casserole or large saucepan.

2 Add the onions to the frying pan and sauté until beginning to turn golden. Add the garlic and cook for a minute or two. Add the juniper berries and flour and stir to combine.

3 Gradually add the wine and bring to the boil, stirring. Pour over the pigeon. Cover with a tight-fitting lid and cook over a low heat for 30 minutes.

4 Stir in the mushrooms and redcurrant jelly or cranberry sauce and continue to cook, covered, over a low heat for 30 minutes, until the meat is very tender and begins to fall from the bone.

5 Serve the pigeon with the vegetables and sauce spooned over. Serve with lots of mashed potato to mop up the fabulous juices.

vegetables

Roast Parsnip Soup

vegetarian

Roasting the parsnips gives this dish a rich flavour. The garnish is optional so, if preferred, you can serve sprinkled with a little chopped parsley. If you can get rapeseed oil, this will add a light flavour and have a deep golden yellow colour with a high burn point, making it ideal for roasting. If you are unable to get rapeseed oil, use olive oil instead.

Ingredients for 2-3

350g/12oz parsnips, peeled
½ small onion, quartered
1 clove garlic, peeled
2 tbsp extra virgin
 rapeseed oil
600ml/1 pint vegetable stock
Salt and freshly ground
 black pepper
Garnish (optional)
 1 small parsnip, peeled
Oil for deep frying

Ingredients for 4-6

700g/1½lb parsnips, peeled
1 small onion, quartered
2 cloves garlic, peeled
4 tbsp extra virgin
 rapeseed oil
1.2 litres/2 pints vegetable
 stock
Salt and freshly ground
 black pepper
Garnish (optional)
 1 parsnip, peeled
Oil for deep frying

1 Preheat the oven to 200°C/400°F/Gas mark 6.

2 Cut the parsnips for the soup into equal-sized chunks. Remove the centre core if the parsnips are large.

3 Place on a roasting tray with the onion and garlic. Sprinkle with the oil and toss to coat. Roast for about 30 minutes or until golden, turning once or twice.

4 Place the roasted vegetables in a saucepan and add half the stock. Bring to the boil, then reduce the heat and simmer for 20 minutes. Season.

5 Purée in a food processor or liquidiser and return to the pan. Add the remaining stock heat gently, stirring. Adjust seasoning to taste.

6 To make the garnish for the soup, slice the parsnip very thinly lengthways (cut in half if it is long) to make long thin strips. Deep-fry in hot fat until crisp and golden. Season and serve piled in a heap on top of the soup.

Pumpkin or Squash Soup

Family Favourite

Autumn is the time for pumpkins, which make delicious soup, and it is in the autumn that you will find the most squashes at the markets. Any autumn summer squash can be used to make this soup; each will give a slightly different taste or texture. Serve this soup with cheese and bacon muffins (see page 163) for a tasty alternative to bread.

Ingredients for 2-4

15g/½oz butter
1 tbsp extra virgin rapeseed
    or olive oil
250g/9oz pumpkin flesh, cut
    into cubes
1 small onion, chopped
1 clove garlic, chopped
225ml/8fl oz vegetable stock
1 sprig fresh thyme
150ml/¼ pint milk
2 thin rashers streaky bacon
Fresh thyme to garnish
Salt and freshly ground
    black pepper

Ingredients for 4-6

25g/1oz butter
2 tbsp extra virgin rapeseed
    or olive oil
500g/1lb 2oz pumpkin flesh,
    cut into cubes
1 onion, chopped
1 clove garlic, chopped
450ml/¾ pint vegetable stock
2 sprigs fresh thyme
300ml/½ pint milk
3 thin rashers streaky bacon
Fresh thyme to garnish
Salt and freshly ground
    black pepper

1 Heat the butter and oil in a large saucepan and fry the pumpkin, onion and garlic over a low heat for 5–10 minutes until softened.

2 Add the stock and thyme. Cover and simmer for 30 minutes.

3 Remove the thyme sprigs. Purée the soup in a liquidiser or food processor and return to the pan.

4 Add the milk and heat gently. Season to taste with salt and pepper.

5 Meanwhile, grill the bacon until very crispy. Serve the soup garnished with a sprinkle of fresh thyme leaves and the crispy bacon.

Coleslaw

This is a handy salad to have in the fridge and it will keep for up to four days. I like the more traditional mayonnaise-based dressing (although I lighten it up with equal quantities of yogurt). You could also use a soured cream dressing, or, if you are watching your waistline, you could try a low calorie vinaigrette dressing instead. Slices of dessert apple, cubes of cheese or nuts can also be added for a more substantial salad.

Ingredients for 3–6:

- ¼ small white cabbage
- 1 carrot
- 1 stick celery
- 2 tbsp mayonnaise
- 2 tbsp wholemilk natural yogurt
- Pinch cayenne pepper
- Salt and freshly ground black pepper

Ingredients for 6–8:

- ½ small white cabbage
- 2 small carrots
- 2 stick celery
- 4 tbsp mayonnaise
- 4 tbsp wholemilk natural yogurt
- Pinch cayenne pepper
- Salt and freshly ground black pepper

1 Remove the centre core from the cabbage and shred finely.

2 Coarsely grate the carrot and thinly slice the celery. Put with the cabbage into a large mixing bowl.

3 Mix together the mayonnaise, yogurt cayenne and seasoning. Pour over the coleslaw and toss until well coated in the dressing.

4 Transfer to a dish to serve.

Mixed Tomato & Onion Salad

Quick and Easy

This is a simple salad which can be made with different varieties of tomatoes when available. Why not try using yellow tomatoes to add extra colour and interest? This is a side salad, but it can easily be made into a main meal salad with the addition of some soft cheese and some fresh salad leaves. Serve with crusty bread.

Ingredients for 2

100g/4oz large tomatoes
2 spring onions
50g/2oz baby plum or cherry
    tomatoes
1 tbsp extra virgin olive oil
½ tsp balsamic vinegar
Salt and freshly ground
    black pepper

Ingredients for 4

225g/8oz large tomatoes
4 spring onions
100g/4oz baby plum or
    cherry tomatoes
2 tbsp extra virgin olive oil
1 tsp balsamic vinegar
Salt and freshly ground
    black pepper

1 Thinly slice the large tomatoes and arrange on a serving plate.

2 Trim and slice the spring onions and sprinkle over the tomato slices.

3 Halve the baby plum or cherry tomatoes and arrange on top.

4 Make a dressing by whisking the remaining ingredients together with a fork and drizzle over the salad. Serve immediately.

Spinach Roulade

Prepare Ahead

This dish is impressive to look at, but easy to make and ideal for a summer buffet table.

700g/1½lb fresh spinach
4 free-range eggs, separated
¼ tsp nutmeg, freshly grated
1 tbsp hard cheese, grated

Filling:

225g/8oz firm tomatoes, seeded and chopped
Salt and freshly ground black pepper
225g/8oz low-fat cream cheese

1 Preheat the oven to 190°C/375°F/Gas mark 5. Grease and line a 20-30 cm/ 8-12 inch Swiss roll tin.

2 Trim any tough stalks from the spinach and place into a saucepan, leaving just the water clinging to the leaves after washing.

3 Cover and cook over a high heat for a few minutes until the spinach wilts, shaking the pan occasionally.

4 Drain well, squeezing out as much moisture as possible. Purée in a food processor. Add the egg yolks, nutmeg and plenty of seasoning. Blend to combine and transfer to a mixing bowl.

5 Whisk the egg white to soft peaks. Fold into the spinach mixture. Pour into the prepared tin and bake for 12–15 minutes until set.

6 To prepare the filling, carefully beat the tomatoes into the cream cheese and season with salt and pepper.

7 Cool the roulade in the tin for 5 minutes. Sprinkle a sheet on non-stick baking parchment with the grated cheese. Turn out the roulade and carefully peel away the lining paper.

8 Spread the filling over the roulade and roll up like a Swiss roll. Serve warm or cold with a salad and crusty bread.

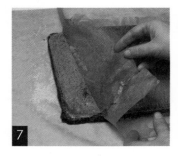

Cauliflower & Broccoli Cheese with Crispy Bacon

A simple supper dish, I enjoy adding broccoli as it gives some colour to an otherwise bland-looking dish. Serve as a side dish or as a light meal. Experiment with the different cheeses you can purchase locally. I like to use a soft creamy cheese in the sauce with a little hard cheese grated for the topping, but you could use a grated hard cheese in the sauce as well.

Ingredients for 2

½ small cauliflower
75g/3oz broccoli florets
15g/½oz butter
15g/½oz plain flour
150ml/¼ pint milk
½ tsp wholegrain mustard
50g/2oz cream/soft cheese
A little sunflower oil
1 shallot, chopped
2 rashers back bacon, from
    outdoor-reared pigs
15g/½oz fresh wholemeal
    breadcrumbs
1 tbsp fresh parsley, chopped
25g/1oz hard cheese, grated
Salt and freshly ground
    black pepper

Ingredients for 4

1 small cauliflower
175g/6oz broccoli florets
25g/1oz butter
25g/1oz plain flour
300ml/½ pint milk
1 tsp wholegrain mustard
100g/4oz cream/soft cheese
A little sunflower oil
2 shallots, chopped
4 rashers back bacon, from
    outdoor-reared pigs
25g/1oz fresh wholemeal
    breadcrumbs
2 tbsp fresh parsley, chopped
50g/2oz hard cheese, grated
Salt and freshly ground
    black pepper

1 Cut the cauliflower into quarters, trim away the excess stem and break each quarter into two.

2 Cook in lightly salted boiling water for 4 minutes, add the broccoli and cook for a further 5 minutes or until tender. Drain and pour into a flameproof dish. Keep warm.

3 Meanwhile, melt the butter in a small saucepan and stir in the flour and cook for a few seconds.

4 Remove from the heat and gradually stir in the milk. Return to the heat and cook, stirring until sauce thickens.

5 Stir in the mustard and cream or soft cheese and cook until the cheese melts. Season to taste and pour over the vegetables.

6 Heat the oil in a small frying pan and add the shallot. Cook for 3–4 minutes until softened. Remove the rind from the bacon and cut into strips. Add the bacon to the pan and cook until beginning to crisp.

7 Mix the bacon mixture with the breadcrumbs, parsley and grated cheese. Season with a little salt and pepper.

8 Sprinkle the breadcrumb mixture over the sauce and place under a preheated grill.Grill until the cheese melts and the crumbs are golden and crispy.

Wild Mushroom Tartlets

Easy Entertaining

If you are lucky, your local farmer's market will have a supply of wild mushrooms in the autumn. Make the most of them while you can. You can also use field mushrooms or button mushrooms. A Yorkshire pudding tin is a shallow tin about 10cm/4 inch across. If you do not have one, you could make twice as many smaller tartlets in a bun tray.

Ingredients for 2

For the pastry cases:

About 1–2 sheets filo pastry
Olive oil for brushing

For the filling:

1 small red onion, peeled
    and cut into thin wedges
1 tbsp olive oil
100g/4oz mixed wild
    mushrooms
25g/1oz butter
1 clove garlic, chopped
A little lemon juice
Salt and freshly ground
    pepper
Soured cream or crème
    fraiche to serve

Ingredients for 4

For the pastry cases:

About 2–3 sheets filo pastry
Olive oil for brushing

For the filling:

2 small red onions, peeled
    and cut into thin wedges
2 tbsp olive oil
225g/8oz mixed wild
    mushrooms
50g/2oz butter
2 cloves garlic, chopped
A little lemon juice
Salt and freshly ground
    black pepper
Soured cream or crème
    fraiche to serve

1 Preheat the oven to 180°C/350°F/Gas mark 4. Cut the sheets of pastry into 12.5cm/5 inch squares.

2 Brush each square with olive oil and place on top of each other until you have a stack of four squares. Use to line the Yorkshire pudding tins.

3 Repeat with the remaining filo to make two (four) shallow pastry cases.

4 Bake in the oven for 8–10 minutes until crisp and golden. Remove from the tins and keep warm.

5 Meanwhile, place the onion wedges on a baking sheet and drizzle with olive oil.

6 Roast in the oven for 15 minutes. Slice or tear the mushrooms into bite-size pieces.

7 Toss with the onion and dot with the butter. Sprinkle over the garlic and season with salt and pepper.

8 Return to the oven for 10–15 minutes until tender. Sprinkle with a little lemon juice.

9 Spoon into the filo pastry cases and serve immediately topped with a generous spoonful of soured cream or crème fraiche.

Creamy Leek & Mushroom Pasta

Family Favourite

You can serve this dish with any pasta shape you have to hand.

Ingredients for 2

1 leek
100g/4oz mushrooms
200g/7oz pasta shapes
1 tbsp olive oil
15g/½oz butter
1 clove garlic, crushed
1 free-range egg
150ml/¼ pint double cream
25g/1oz hard cheese, grated
**Salt and freshly ground
    black pepper**

Ingredients for 4

2 leeks
225g/8oz mushrooms
400g/14oz pasta shapes
2 tbsp olive oil
25g/1oz butter
1 clove garlic, crushed
2 free-range eggs
300ml/½ pint double cream
50g/2oz hard cheese, grated
**Salt and freshly ground
    black pepper**

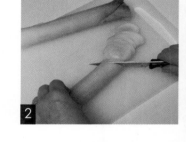

1 Trim the leeks, slice on a slight diagonal, wash and rinse well. Slice the mushrooms.

2 Cook the pasta in plenty of lightly salted boiling water for 10 minutes, or as directed on the packet.

3 Meanwhile, heat the oil and butter in a large frying pan and sauté the leeks and mushrooms for 10 minutes until soft. Stir in the garlic and sauté for 1 minute.

4 Beat the eggs in a bowl, then beat in the cream and stir in the cheese.

5 When the pasta is nearly cooked, stir the cream mixture into the leeks and mushrooms, and cook very gently, stirring until piping hot. Do not allow to boil. Season to taste.

6 Drain the pasta, pour over the sauce and toss to combine.

Sprouting Broccoli with Creamy Lemon Sauce

Easy Entertaining

Sprouting broccoli is an attractive vegetable which is perfect steamed with just a knob of butter. For something a little more special, try serving with a simple sauce.

Ingredients for 2

250g/9oz purple sprouting
    broccoli
1 tsp lemon juice
¼ tsp grated unwaxed
    lemon zest
75ml/2½fl oz fromage frais
    or crème fraiche
Grated nutmeg

Ingredients for 4

500g/1lb 2oz purple
    sprouting broccoli
1 tbsp lemon juice
½ tsp grated unwaxed
    lemon zest
150ml/¼ pint fromage frais
    or crème fraiche
Grated nutmeg

1 Trim the base of the broccoli. Steam for 10 minutes until just tender.

2 Meanwhile combine the lemon juice, zest and fromage frais or crème fraiche in a small bowl.

3 Drain the broccoli and place on a warm serving plate. Drizzle the sauce over and sprinkle with nutmeg. Serve immediately.

Asparagus with Garlic Cream

Easy Entertaining

Asparagus has a very short season and to my mind, English asparagus has the best flavour so it is worth looking out for it in late spring. It is fabulous steamed or gently poached and served with a knob of butter and a sprinkling of black pepper. Alternatively, why not try this simple-to-prepare side dish which is delicious served with plain grilled fish or meat, or as a simple starter.

Ingredients for 2

250g/9oz asparagus spears
100ml/3½fl oz double cream
1 clove garlic, peeled and crushed
Salt and white pepper
Chopped fresh parsley

Ingredients for 4

500g/1lb 2oz asparagus spears
200ml/7fl oz double cream
2 cloves garlic, peeled and crushed
Salt and white pepper
Chopped fresh parsley

1 Trim the asparagus ends, at the point at which the stem breaks easily. Bring a frying pan of water to a gentle simmer and add a little salt.

2 Add the asparagus, placing the pan slightly off-centre on the hob so that the stems are over the heat and the tips just off the heat. Simmer gently for 5–6 minutes until just tender.

3 Meanwhile, place the cream and garlic in a saucepan and bring to the boil. Reduce the heat and simmer for 5 minutes until thickened slightly.

4 When the asparagus is cooked, drain well and serve with the cream sauce poured over.

Celeriac & Potato Mash

Quick and Easy

Celeriac has a wonderful flavour, reminiscent of celery. It is an ugly root vegetable sometimes marketed as 'the ugly one' but don't let this put you off. It makes the most wonderful mash.

Ingredients for 2

250g/9oz celeriac
200g/7oz floury potatoes
25g/1oz butter
3 tbsp milk
**Salt and freshly ground
   black pepper**

Ingredients for 4

500g/1lb 2oz celeriac
400g/14oz floury potatoes
50g/2oz butter
6 tbsp milk
**Salt and freshly ground
   black pepper**

1 Peel and cut the celeriac and potatoes into 2.5cm/ 1 inch chunks.

2 Cook the potatoes and celeriac in lightly salted boiling water for 10–12 minutes or until just tender.

3 Drain well. Heat the butter and milk in a small pan until just simmering. Add to the vegetables and mash well. Season to taste and serve immediately.

Braised Celery with Almonds

If you think celery is only for eating raw when on a diet, think again. Celery can also be served as a very flavoursome vegetable. If liked, a little bacon can be added to the almond mixture.

Ingredients for 2

½ **bunch celery**
15g/½oz **butter**
1 **small onion, chopped**
25g/1oz **flaked almonds**
¼ tsp **celery salt**
1 tbsp **fresh parsley, chopped**

Ingredients for 4

1 **bunch celery**
25g/1oz **butter**
1 **onion, chopped**
50g/2oz **flaked almonds**
½ tsp **celery salt**
2 tbsp **fresh parsley, chopped**

1 Trim, wash and cut the celery into 7.5cm/3 inch lengths. A nail brush is ideal for cleaning celery if it is very dirty. Blanch in boiling water for 2 minutes. Drain reserving 90ml/3fl oz (150ml/¼ pint) of the water.

2 Heat the butter in a large sauté pan or frying pan with a lid and sauté the onion until softened.

3 Add the flaked almonds and fry until golden. Pour in the reserved liquid.

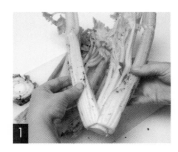

4 Add the celery to the pan, sprinkle over the celery salt and cover with a tight-fitting lid. Simmer gently for 20–25 minutes until the celery is tender and most of the liquid has evaporated.

5 Serve sprinkled with parsley.

Sautéed Chard with Shallots & Garlic

Chard is a member of the beet family which is grown primarily for its stem, which may be white or red and has a delicate unique flavour. The stems and leaves can be cooked separately. Use the leaves in soup or stews and serve the stem as a vegetable in its own right, or as here, sauté the two together to give a fabulous side dish.

Ingredients for 2

200g/7oz chard
1 tbsp olive oil
15g/½oz butter
2 shallots, chopped
1 clove garlic, chopped
½ tbsp red wine vinegar
Salt and freshly ground
    black pepper

Ingredients for 4

400g/14oz chard
2 tbsp olive oil
25g/1oz butter
4 shallots, chopped
2 cloves garlic, chopped
1 tbsp red wine vinegar
Salt and freshly ground
    black pepper

1 Cut the stem from the leaves and slice thickly.

2 Tear or cut the leaves into pieces.

3 Heat the oil and butter in a large frying pan and gently sauté the shallot until softened. Add the garlic and chard stems and sauté for 3–4 minutes until the stems are beginning to soften, stirring frequently.

4 Add the leaves and continue to sauté for 3–4 minutes until the vegetable is tender.

5 Pour in the red wine vinegar and season with salt and pepper. Toss in the pan and serve.

Roast Jerusalem Artichokes

Despite their names, Jerusalem and globe artichokes are not related. Choose firm unbruised Jerusalem artichokes. They tend to be irregular in shape, but try to select artichokes of a similar size.

Ingredients for 2

250g/9oz Jerusalem artichokes
A little lemon juice
1 tbsp olive oil
½ tbsp fresh rosemary, chopped
½ tsp fresh thyme, chopped
Salt and freshly ground black pepper

Ingredients for 4

500g/1lb 2oz Jerusalem artichokes
A little lemon juice
2 tbsp olive oil
1 tbsp fresh rosemary, chopped
1 tsp fresh thyme, chopped
Salt and freshly ground black pepper

1 Preheat the oven to 190°C/375°F/Gas mark 5.

2 Peel the Jerusalem artichokes and drop into a bowl of water to which a little lemon juice has been added.

3 Remove from the water, shaking off the excess. Cut into equal-sized pieces and toss with the olive oil, rosemary and thyme.

4 Spread out in a single layer in a shallow roasting dish and sprinkle with salt and pepper.

5 Roast for about 40–45 minutes depending on the size of the pieces or until just tender when pierced with a skewer.

6 Serve immediately.

Courgette Cake

This is a variation on the more familiar carrot cake and, like carrots, the courgette adds sweetness to the cake as well as giving it a fabulous moist texture. You can substitute half the courgettes with carrots if preferred.

Ingredients for 1 cake

3 free-range eggs
75g/3oz golden caster sugar
150g/5oz self-raising flour
225g/8oz courgettes, trimmed and grated
25g/1oz butter, melted

Frosting:

175g/6oz full-fat cream cheese
1 tbsp lemon or orange juice
75g/3oz icing sugar

1 Preheat the oven to 180°C/350°F/Gas mark 4. Lightly oil and line the base of a 20cm/8 inch round cake tin.

2 Place the eggs and sugar in a large mixing bowl and whisk until very pale and thick.

3 Fold in the courgettes. Carefully fold in the flour. Drizzle over the melted butter and fold in.

4 Pour into the prepared cake tin and bake for 25–35 minutes or until springy to the touch. Cool in the tin for 5 minutes before transferring to a wire rack to cool completely.

5 Beat together the cheese, lemon juice and icing sugar until just combined. Spread over the top of the cake. Serve cut into wedges.

cheese
and dairy

Goat Cheese & Leek Tarts

I find the mild flavour of leeks works well with goats cheese. Serve with a rocket and cherry tomato salad for a great lunch time dish.

Ingredients for 3:

90g/3½oz plain flour
40g/1½oz butter
Cold water to mix
1 tbsp olive oil
1 leek, washed and sliced
1 free-range egg
75ml/2½fl oz milk
50g/2oz fresh, medium-fat,
   soft goat cheese
Salt and freshly ground
   black pepper

Ingredients for 6:

175g/6oz plain flour
75g/3oz butter
Cold water to mix
2 tbsp olive oil
2 leeks, washed and sliced
2 free-range eggs
150ml/¼ pint milk
150g/5oz fresh, medium-fat,
   soft goat cheese
Salt and freshly ground
   black pepper

1 Sift the flour into a mixing bowl and rub in the butter until the mixture resembles fine breadcrumbs.

2 Add enough water to mix to a soft dough.

3 Roll out the pastry on a lightly floured surface and line three (six) 15cm/6 inch flan tins. Prick the base of each pastry case with a fork.

4 Chill for 20 minutes. Preheat the oven to 200°C/400°F/Gas mark 6.

5 Line each pastry case with baking parchment, fill with baking beans and bake for 10 minutes.

6 Remove the paper and beans and bake for another 5 minutes until the pastry is crisp and golden. Reduce the temperature to 180°C/350°F/Gas mark 4.

7 Heat the oil in a small frying pan and sauté the leeks until soft. Spread over the base of the pastry cases. Place teaspoons or slices of the goat cheese over the top.

8 Beat together the eggs and milk until well combined. Season well. Pour into the pastry cases. Bake for 20–25 minutes until the filling is just set. Serve hot or cold.

Sour Cream, Cheese & Sun-blushed Tomato Dip

Quick and Easy

Sun-blushed tomatoes are tomatoes that have been semi-dried, producing a sweet, intense flavour. You may be able to get these at your farmer's market, alternatively, you can make your own by roasting halved cherry tomatoes in a low oven. Sun-dried tomatoes in olive oil can be used but the flavour is much stronger, so use fewer.

Ingredients for 2

100g/4oz cream cheese
3 tbsp soured cream
25g/1oz sun-blushed tomatoes
2 spring onions, chopped
1 tsp pesto
Bread or vegetables for dipping
Basil to garnish (optional)

Ingredients for 4

200g/7oz cream cheese
90ml/3fl oz soured cream
50g/2oz sun-blushed tomatoes
4 spring onions, chopped
2 tsp pesto
Bread or vegetables for dipping
Basil to garnish (optional)

1 Combine the cream cheese and soured cream until smooth.

2 Chop the tomatoes and beat into the cheese mixture.

3 Stir in the spring onions and pesto. Transfer to a serving bowl and garnish with basil if desired.

4 Serve with bread or crudités for dipping.

Farmhouse Cheese Fondue

Easy Entertaining

Fondues have become fashionable again, having first put in an appearance in this country in the 1970s. Originating in the Alps, this has been given the farmer's market twist and is made with good quality English cheese. It tastes just as good.

Ingredients for 2

1 clove garlic
75ml/2½fl oz dry cider
225g/8oz farmhouse
   Cheddar, grated
1 tsp cornflour
1 tbsp sherry
Ground white pepper
Pinch grated nutmeg
Pinch paprika
To serve – day old crusty
   bread cut into cubes

Ingredients for 4

1 clove garlic
150ml/¼ pint dry cider
450g/1lb farmhouse
   Cheddar, grated
1 tbsp corn flour
2 tbsp sherry
Ground white pepper
Pinch grated nutmeg
Pinch paprika
To serve – day old crusty
   bread cut into cubes

1 Rub the inside of a fondue pan or heavy-based saucepan with a cut clove of garlic. Pour the cider into the pan and heat gently until almost simmering.

2 Gradually add the cheese, stirring constantly as you do so. At first the cheese will be a solid mass in the pan with a milky liquid around it. As the cheese warms up, the liquid can be blended into the melted cheese.

3 Once the mixture is smooth, blend the cornflour and sherry together and add to the pan. Continue to cook gently for a further 1–2 minutes, stirring constantly.

4 Season to taste with the pepper, nutmeg and paprika. Serve at the table over a fondue burner set low. Use bread cubes for dipping.

Goat Cheese Salad with a Slow-roasted Tomato Dressing

This is a lovely summer salad. The dressing will keep for about a week in the refrigerator.

Slow-roasted Tomato Dressing:

225g/8oz cherry tomatoes, quartered
5 tbsp extra virgin olive oil
1 clove garlic, chopped
2 tbsp balsamic vinegar
Salt and freshly ground black pepper

Ingredients for 2

Salad:

**2 slices Ciabatta or other
    continental-style bread**
1 tbsp olive oil
½ clove garlic
**About 50g/2oz young local
    goat cheese**
**40g/1½oz mixed salad
leaves**
**2 tbsp slow-roasted tomato
    dressing**

Ingredients for 4

Salad:

**4 slices Ciabatta bread or
    other continental-style
    bread**
2 tbsp olive oil
1 clove garlic, halved
**About 100g/4oz young local
    goat cheese**
75g/3oz mixed salad leaves
**4 tbsp slow-roasted tomato
    dressing**

1 To make the dressing, preheat the oven to 170°C/325°F/Gas mark 3. Arrange the tomatoes on a baking sheet. Drizzle with a little of the olive oil. Season with salt and pepper and scatter the garlic on top. Roast for 25 minutes.

2 Toss the roasted tomatoes with the remaining oil and balsamic vinegar. Allow to cool.

3 Brush the oil on both sides of the bread slices and toast until just golden. Rub both sides of the bread with the garlic halves and set aside.

4 Cut the goat cheese into 2 slices (4 slices) and place on top of the toasted bread. Grill until cheese softens and begins to melt.

5 Place the bread slices onto serving plates and top with the salad leaves.

6 Spoon the tomato dressing over the top and serve immediately.

Crème Caramel

Prepare Ahead

If you are lucky enough to have a dairy farmer who has Guernsey cows use this milk, as it has a higher fat content than milk from the more common Frisian cow. Guernsey milk gives a creamier, richer flavour to this classic dessert. Whatever you use, I find this a delicious end to a meal. It is difficult to make the caramel in smaller quantities than this, but the desserts will keep a couple of days in the refrigerator.

Ingredients for 4

1 vanilla pod
450ml/¾ pint whole milk preferably from Guernsey cows
75g/3oz golden granulated sugar
3 free-range eggs
25g/1oz golden caster sugar

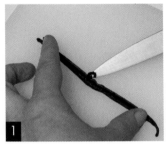

1 Split the vanilla pod in half lengthways and scrape out the seeds with the tip of a knife. Place the vanilla pod, seeds and milk in a saucepan and heat until beginning to bubble. Set aside to infuse whilst making the caramel.

2 Place the granulated sugar in a small saucepan with 3 tablespoons of water and heat gently, stirring until the sugar dissolves.

3 Once all the sugar has dissolved, increase the heat and boil until the sugar turns a rich caramel colour. Watch the syrup constantly as it can burn very quickly.

4 When a rich, golden caramel has been reached, immediately pour a little into the base of 4 warm ramekin dishes.

5 Preheat the oven to 150°C/300°F/Gas mark 2. Beat together the eggs and caster sugar until well combined. Bring back the milk to almost boiling point and remove the vanilla pod. This can be rinsed and used again

or popped into a jar of sugar to make vanilla sugar.

6 Gradually whisk the hot milk into the eggs and sugar. Strain the mixture through a fine sieve and pour into the ramekin dishes.

7 Place the ramekin dishes in a roasting tin and pour boiling water into the tin to come half way up the side of the dishes. Bake for 20 minutes or until set.

8 Remove from the water and allow to cool. Chill until required. Turn out onto small dishes to serve.

Coffee Crème Brulées

Easy Entertaining

I always use Fair Trade coffee. Fair Trade is a scheme that has been set up to ensure fair pay to growers and workers in the developing world.

Ingredients for 6

450ml/¾ pint double cream
200ml/7fl oz strong black coffee
8 free-range egg yolks
50g/2oz golden caster sugar
1 tsp cornflour
50g/2oz Demerara sugar

1 Preheat the oven to 170°C/325°F/Gas mark 3.

2 Place the cream and coffee in a small saucepan and heat gently, stirring until just beginning to simmer. Do not allow to boil.

3 Whisk the egg yolks with the caster sugar and cornflour, then gradually whisk in the hot cream and coffee mixture.

4 Pour into ramekin dishes. Place in a roasting tin. Put enough boiling water into the tin to come halfway up the sides of the dishes.

5 Bake for 25 minutes or until the cream is just set. Allow to cool then chill completely in the refrigerator.

6 Sprinkle the Demerara sugar over the top of each cream and place under a hot grill, or use a blow torch to melt and caramelise the sugar.

7 Chill again before serving.

Mini Pavlovas with Yogurt & Fruit

The choice of berries is up to you, but blueberries and strawberries are packed with the antioxidant vitamin C, vital for a healthy diet.

Ingredients for 6

2 egg whites
150g/5oz golden caster sugar
½ tsp vanilla essence
¼ tsp vinegar
50g/2oz ground toasted hazelnuts
4 tbsp strawberry or raspberry jam
1 tbsp orange flavoured liqueur or water
300g/10½oz thick sheep's yogurt or Greek-style yogurt
Fresh fruit to serve

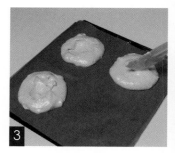

1 Preheat the oven to 150°C/300°F/Gas mark 2. Line a baking sheet with non-stick baking parchment.

2 Whisk the egg whites until stiff. Gradually whisk in the caster sugar. Carefully fold in the vanilla essence, vinegar and hazelnuts.

3 Pile the meringue into six mounds on the baking sheet and spread out with the back of a spoon to make 10–12cm/4–5 inch circles with a slight dip in the centre. Make sure they are not too close together.

4 Bake in the oven for 45–60 minutes until dry and crisp on the outside. Allow to cool.

5 To serve, carefully transfer to serving plates. Warm the jam with the orange liqueur or water stirring to combine.

6 Pile the yogurt into the centre of the meringue and arrange some fruit on top. Drizzle over the jam and serve.

Curd Cheese Tart

Prepare Ahead

This is a cross between a baked egg custard tart and a cheese cake. It is a lovely dessert that can be served on its own or with summer berries. Choose a soft curd or cream cheese with a mild flavour.

Serves 6-8

Pastry:
100g/4oz butter
225g/8oz plain flour
1 tbsp golden caster sugar
About 1–2 tbsp cold water
to mix

Filling:
350g/12oz curd or cream
cheese
3 free-range eggs, separated
75g/3oz golden caster sugar
1 tsp vanilla essence
75g/3oz sultanas (optional)
Freshly grated nutmeg

1 To make the pastry case, cut the butter into cubes and rub into the flour until the mixture resembles fine breadcrumbs. Stir in the sugar, and add enough cold water to mix to a soft dough.

2 Roll out the pastry and use to line a 23cm/9 inch flan or cake tin about 3–5cm /1½–2cm deep. Prick the base with a fork and chill for 20 minutes.

3 Preheat the oven to 200°C/400°F/Gas mark 6.

4 Line the pastry case with greaseproof paper and fill with baking beans and bake

for 10 minutes. Remove the paper and beans and bake for 10 minutes. Reduce the oven temperature to 180°C/350°F/ Gas mark 4.

5 To make the filling, beat together the cheese, egg yolks, sugar and vanilla essence until well combined. Stir in the sultanas if using.

6 Whisk the egg whites and fold into the cheese mixture. Pour into the pastry case and generously sprinkle with nutmeg.

7 Bake for 35 to 45 minutes or until the filling is just set. Cool before serving.

Buttermilk Scones

Family Favourite

These are just the thing for a classic cream tea. Serve these 'light as a feather' scones with clotted cream and strawberry jam, bought from your local farmer's market of course.

Ingredients for about 12

350g/12oz self-raising flour
75g/3oz butter, cut into small cubes
2 tbsp golden caster sugar
About 175–200ml/6–7fl oz buttermilk
Beaten egg or milk to glaze

To serve:

Clotted cream
Strawberry or other good fruit jam

1 Preheat the oven to 220°C/425°F/Gas mark 7. Lightly grease a baking sheet.

2 Sift the flour into a bowl and rub in the butter with your fingertips. Stir in the sugar.

3 Mix in enough buttermilk to form a soft dough.

4 Turn out onto a floured work surface and lightly knead. Roll out the dough until about 2.5cm/1 inch thick. Cut out the scones with a 7cm/3 inch round cookie cutter.

5 Re-roll any trimmings and cut out more scones. Place on a lightly greased baking sheet. Brush the tops with beaten egg or milk to glaze.

6 Bake for 18–20 minutes until golden. Cool on a wire rack.

7 Serve split in half and filled with clotted cream and jam.

fruits

Sparkling Summer Fruit Jelly

Easy Entertaining

The sparkling wine gives this dessert a very special kick. The bubbles really do seem to get trapped in the jelly. You can vary the fruits according to what is available.

Ingredients for 6-8

350g/12oz strawberries
100g/4oz redcurrants or blackcurrants
225g/8oz raspberries
150g/5oz packet of strawberry or raspberry jelly
About 300ml/½ pint sparkling white or rosé wine

1 Hull the strawberries and halve or quarter if large. Strip the currants from their stalks, rinse the fruit and drain well. Place in a 1.2 litre/2 pint jelly mould, bowl or 900g/2lb loaf tin.

2 Break the jelly into cubes and dissolve in 150ml/¼ pint boiling water. Make the jelly up to 600ml/1 pint with the sparkling wine.

3 Pour the jelly over the fruit and chill in the refrigerator for at least 4 hours, or until set.

4 To serve, dip the tin into hot water briefly for a few seconds, making sure that no water gets onto the jelly. Turn out onto a plate, giving the jelly mould a good shake until it drops out. If required, you can dip it in hot water again – but not for too long or the jelly will melt.

Strawberries with Lavender Shortcakes

Easy Entertaining

The lavender gives these biscuits an unusual flavour which complements the strawberries perfectly. You could try chopped rosemary instead.

Ingredients for 6

100g/4oz butter, softened
50g/2oz golden caster sugar
Few sprigs of fresh or dried lavender
1 free-range egg yolk
150g/5oz plain flour
350g/12oz strawberries
1 tbsp raspberry- or orange-flavoured liqueur (optional)

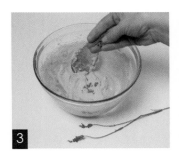

1 Preheat the oven to 190°C /375°F/Gas mark 5. Lightly grease two baking sheets.

2 Beat the butter and sugar together until light and fluffy.

3 Remove the lavender flowers from the stems and beat in with the egg yolk.

4 Add the flour and mix to a soft dough. Roll out the dough on a lightly floured surface to 3mm/⅛in thick. Stamp out twelve 7.5cm/3 inch rounds with a cookie cutter.

5 Transfer to the baking sheets and bake for 8–10 minutes until golden. Allow to cool for a few minutes before transferring to a wire rack to cool completely.

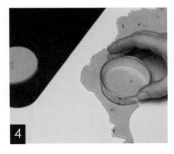

6 Wash and hull the strawberries. Slice two-thirds of the strawberries and place in a mixing bowl. Purée the remaining strawberries with the liqueur (if using), and push through a sieve to remove the seeds. Stir the puree into the strawberry slices.

7 Place one biscuit on a plate and top with ⅙ of the strawberry mixture. Top with another biscuit

8 Repeat with the remaining biscuits and strawberries. Any remaining strawberry purée can be drizzled onto the plate for decoration.

Old-fashioned Trifle

Family Favourite

Trifles of my childhood consisted of layers of fruit jelly and firm blancmange and whilst I loved them at the time, I was yet to be introduced to the softer, fruitier, old fashioned trifles which I adore.

Ingredients for 6

100g/4oz slightly stale Madeira cake
150g/5oz raspberries
150g/5oz strawberries
2–3 tbsp sherry

Custard:
450ml/¾ pint milk
1 tbsp cornflour
1–2 tbsp golden caster sugar
3 free-range egg yolks
1 free-range egg
1 tsp vanilla essence

Topping:
300ml/½ pint double cream
1 tbsp flaked almonds, lightly toasted
2 tbsp seedless raspberry jam

1 Arrange pieces of cake in the bottom of a glass serving bowl. Scatter over the raspberries and strawberries. Drizzle the sherry over the fruit.

2 To make the custard, mix a little of the milk with cornflour and sugar to form a smooth paste in a heat-proof mixing bowl.

3 Add the egg yolks, whole egg and vanilla essence and whisk until smooth.

4 Heat the remaining milk until almost boiling. Gradually whisk into the egg mixture. Place the bowl over a pan of gently simmering water and cook, stirring constantly until the custard thickens.

5 Remove from the heat. Cover with a sheet of dampened greaseproof paper and allow to cool.

6 When the custard is cold, pour over the fruit. Lightly whip the double cream and carefully spread over the custard. Sprinkle the nuts on top. Warm the jam, thin with a little water if required, and drizzle over the top. Chill the trifle until served.

Blackcurrant Cheesecake

Family Favourite

Serves 8

225g/8oz oat biscuits
75g/3oz butter
350g/12oz full-fat or medium-fat cream cheese
100g/4oz golden caster sugar
225g/8oz Greek-style or wholemilk yogurt
300ml/½ pint double cream
1 tsp vanilla essence
1 tbsp gelatine

Topping:

250g/9oz blackcurrants
25g/1oz golden caster sugar
2 tsp arrowroot

1 Place the biscuits in a plastic bag and crush with a rolling pin.

2 Melt the butter and stir in the biscuits. Press into the base of a 23cm/9 inch loose-bottom or springform cake tin.

3 Beat together the cream cheese and sugar until well combined, then beat in the yogurt. Whip the cream into soft peaks and fold it into the cream cheese mixture with the vanilla essence.

4 Sprinkle the gelatine over 3 tablespoons of water and leave until spongy. Place in a pan of hot water or in a microwave for about 15 seconds and stir until dissolved. Fold into the cheese mixture.

5 Pour into the prepared tin and chill until set.

6 To make the topping, mix together the blackcurrants, sugar and arrowroot with 2 tablespoons of water in a small saucepan and heat gently, stirring until the sugar dissolves and the mixture thickens. Allow to cool covered with dampened non-stick baking parchment.

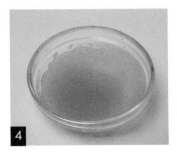

7 Carefully remove the cheesecake from the tin and spread the blackcurrant mixture over the top.

Blackberry & Apple Crumble

Family Favourite

I couldn't leave out a recipe for one of my favourite autumn puddings. I grew up in the country and the fruit for this dessert came from our garden. Now I live in town, the fruit comes from the farmer's market, but the flavour is just as good and I look forward to the first crumble of the autumn.

Ingredients for 4–6

500g/1lb 2oz cooking apples, peeled, cored and thickly sliced
350g/12oz blackberries
50g/ 2oz golden caster sugar

For the topping:

90g/3½oz butter, cut into cubes
150g/5oz plain flour
50g/2oz rolled oats
4 tbsp Demerara sugar

1 Preheat the oven to 200°C/400°F/Gas mark 6.

2 Layer the apples and blackberries in a shallow pie dish, sprinkling each layer with caster sugar.

3 To make the topping, rub the butter into the flour until the mixture resembles coarse breadcrumbs.

4 Stir in the oats and Demerara sugar.

5 Sprinkle the topping over the fruit and bake for 35–40 minutes or until the top is crisp and golden.

Rhubarb Rice Custards

Fresh, tender shoots of rhubarb first appear in spring. Later they are thicker, but still have a great flavour. Rhubarb is delicious used in crumbles and of course combines well with custard. Here, rhubarb and custard has been given a very modern twist.

Ingredients for 2

225g/8oz rhubarb, cut into
   2.5cm/1 inch lengths
1 tbsp orange juice
50g/2oz golden caster sugar
100g/4oz cooked rice
1 free-range egg
225ml/8fl oz milk

Ingredients for 4

450g/1lb rhubarb, cut into
   2.5cm/1 inch lengths
2 tbsp orange juice
100g/4oz golden caster sugar
200g/7oz cooked rice
2 free-range eggs
450ml/¾ pint milk

1 Place the rhubarb in a small pan with the orange juice and 2 tablespoons (4 tablespoons) of the sugar. Cover and cook over a low heat for 5–10 minutes until just soft. Spoon into individual ovenproof dishes.

2 Preheat the oven to 170°C/325°F/Gas mark 3. Divide the rice between the dishes.

3 Place the eggs in a mixing bowl and whisk in the remaining sugar, until dissolved.

4 Stir in the milk and pour over the rice.

5 Place the dishes in a roasting tin. Bring a kettle of water to the boil and pour the water into the roasting tin until it reaches halfway up the dishes.

6 Bake for 30–40 minutes until just set. Serve hot or cold.

Poached Pears

Low Fat

If the pears you buy are a good shape, you can poach them whole. Simply extend the cooking time a little. As pears from the market can vary in shape, I prefer to cut them in half to poach. This recipe can also be made using cider in place of the red wine and port.

Ingredients for 3:

75ml/2½fl oz red wine
75ml/2½fl oz port
50g/2oz golden caster sugar
1 tsp lemon juice
1 cinnamon stick
Pinch grated nutmeg
Pinch ground cloves
3 firm pears
Whipped cream to serve

Ingredients for 6:

150ml/¼ pint red wine
150ml/¼ pint port
100g/4oz golden caster sugar
1 tbsp lemon juice
1 cinnamon stick
¼ tsp grated nutmeg
Pinch ground cloves
6 firm pears
Whipped cream to serve

1 Place the wine, port, sugar, lemon juice and spices into a saucepan and heat gently, stirring until the sugar dissolves.

2 Peel the pears and cut in half. Scoop out the core with a teaspoon. Place in the liquid in the pan.

3 Cover and simmer gently for 20 minutes, or until the pears are tender. Spoon the syrup over the pears a few times during cooking.

4 Remove the pears with a draining spoon, and set aside. Remove the cinnamon stick and discard.

5 Return the pan to the heat and reduce the liquid until syrupy by boiling rapidly.

6 Pour over the pears. Serve hot, or cool and chill in the refrigerator, spooning the syrup over the pears from time to time.

7 Serve the pears with whipped cream.

Cherry Cream Pie

Easy Entertaining

A humble cherry pie turns into a spectacular dessert with the addition of cream and rum during the cooking. Apples or pears could also be used as a filling, with the addition of cream and brandy.

Ingredients for 4–6

Pastry:

175g/6oz plain flour
75g/3oz butter, cut into cubes
2 tbsp golden caster sugar, plus extra to dust
1–2 tbsp cold water
Milk to glaze

Filling:

900g/2lb cherries, stoned
50g/2oz light muscovado sugar
100ml/3½fl oz double cream
3 tbsp rum

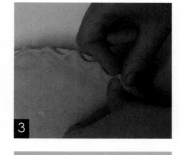

1 To make the pastry, sift the flour into a bowl. Rub the butter into the flour until the mixture resembles fine breadcrumbs. Stir in the sugar and add enough water to mix to a soft dough.

2 Layer the cherries and sugar in a pie dish. Roll out the pastry until about 5cm/2 inch wider than the pie dish. Cut a strip from around the pastry. Dampen the rim of the pie dish and press the strip of pastry onto the rim.

3 Dampen the strip and cover the dish with the remaining pastry. Trim and pinch the edges of the pastry to seal. Carefully remove a 5cm/2 inch circle of pastry from the centre of the pie. Chill for 20 minutes.

4 Preheat the oven to 200°C/400°F/Gas mark 6. Brush the pastry with a little milk and sprinkle with a little caster sugar. Bake for 20–25 minutes or until the pastry is pale golden

5 Place the cream and rum in a small saucepan and heat gently until the cream begins to bubble around the edges of the pan. Do not allow to boil.

6 Carefully pour the cream mixture into the pie through the hole in the pastry.

7 Return to the oven and bake for a further 10 minutes until the pastry is crisp and golden.

Plum and Coconut Tart

Freezer Friendly

With the odd exception, the plums that you can buy in the supermarkets all year round tend to be tasteless compared to our own English plums, which are available in early autumn. They are one of my favourite fruits, and all the more special for their seasonal availability. My fruit bowl is always piled high with them when they are in season. But they also make fabulous pies and tarts, and this one is no exception.

Serves 6-8

225g/8oz plain flour
100g/4oz butter or sunflower margarine
A little cold water

Topping:
450g/1lb Plums

Filling:

100g/4oz butter, softened
100g/4oz light muscovado sugar
2 free-range eggs, lightly beaten
50g/2oz self-raising flour
75g/3oz desiccated coconut

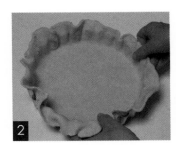

1 Place the flour into a bowl, cut the butter into small chunks and rub in with your fingertips until the mixture resembles fine breadcrumbs. Add enough water to mix to a firm dough.

2 Roll out the pastry and use to line a 23cm/9 inch flan dish or tin. Prick the base all over and chill for 15 minutes.

3 Preheat the oven to 200°C/400°F/Gas mark 6. Line the pastry case with baking parchment or greaseproof paper and fill with baking beans.

4 Bake blind for 10 minutes, remove beans and paper and bake for 10 minutes.

Reduce the oven temperature to 180°C/350°F/Gas mark 4.

5 To make the filling, beat together the butter and sugar until light and fluffy. Gradually beat in the eggs. Stir in the flour and coconut.

6 Cut the plums in half and remove the stones. Spoon the coconut mixture into the pastry case and level the top.

7 Arrange the plum halves cut-side down on top. Bake in the centre of the oven for 30–40 minutes until the coconut mixture is risen and golden.

8 Allow to cool before cutting into wedges to serve.

Greengage Jam

Prepare Ahead

Greengages are small green plums named after Sir William Gage who brought them back from France in the 18th century. They make fabulous jam which has a good set. They can also be poached or used to make pies, as well as being delicious eaten raw. Look out for them around September as their season is quite short.

Ingredients for approx 2kg/4lb:

1.35kg/3lb greengages
300ml/½ pint water
1.35kg/3lb jam sugar

1 Wash the greengages, halve, and remove the stones.

2 Put the fruit into a large pan, with the water and simmer gently for 20 minutes until beginning to soften.

3 Stir in the sugar and cook over a very low heat, stirring frequently until the sugar has dissolved.

4 Increase the heat and boil the jam until setting point has been reached (about 10 minutes).

5 Test for setting point by placing a small amount of the jam on a cold plate and allowing it to cool. Push gently with your finger. The surface of the jam will crinkle if setting point has been reached. Do not continue to cook the jam whilst testing for setting. If the setting point has not been reached, return to the heat and boil for a few more minutes before testing again.

6 Once setting point has been reached, pour into sterilised jars, label and seal.

Cook's Note
To sterilise jars, wash them well in hot, soapy water and rinse out. Place the wet jars on a baking tray and place in the oven at 150°C/300°F/Gas mark 2 for 10 minutes. Fill the jars whilst still hot to the top and cover with a disc of waxed paper, waxed side down, making sure it is flat on the surface. Seal the jars and allow to cool.

Quince & Apple Chutney

Prepare Ahead

This is a fabulous chutney served with cheese or cold meats. Store in the refrigerator or in a cool, dark place to maximise its keeping qualities.

Ingredients for 1.3–1.8kg/3–4lb

700g/1½lb quince
450g/1lb cooking apples
225g/8oz onion, chopped
4 sticks celery, chopped
350g/12oz firm tomatoes, chopped *(under-ripe tomatoes are fine)*
175g/6oz raisins
75ml/2½fl oz water
450g/1lb unrefined Demerara sugar
1 tbsp caraway seeds
600ml/1 pint white wine vinegar

1 Peel, core and chop the quince and apples.

2 Place the quince, apple, onion, celery, tomatoes and raisins in a large pan with the water and cook gently for 20–30 minutes until the fruit and vegetables are very soft.

3 Add the sugar and vinegar and cook. Stir until the sugar dissolves. Continue to cook, stirring occasionally, until the chutney is very thick (about 2 hours). Use a long-handled wooden spoon to stir the chutney as it tends to splatter when stirred. The mixture is very hot, so it is a good idea to protect your hands with a tea towel or oven gloves to do this.

4 Allow to cool slightly. Pour into sterilised jars, seal and label.

Cook's Note

To sterilise jars, wash them well in hot, soapy water and rinse out. Place the wet jars on a baking tray and put in the oven at 150°C/300°F/Gas mark 2 for 10 minutes. Fill the jars whilst still hot to the top and cover with a disc of waxed paper, waxed side down, making sure it is flat on the surface. Seal jars and allow to cool.

Blue Cheese, Pear & Walnut Salad

Easy Entertaining

The flavours and textures combine well in this fabulous salad. Use a blue cheese that is local to you. In some areas, you may even find walnuts at your local farmer's market.

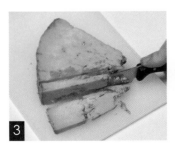

Ingredients for 2

1 pear, peeled cored and sliced
Little lemon juice
25g/1oz watercress or rocket leaves
2 tomatoes, seeded and chopped
1 tbsp sherry vinegar
2 tbsp extra virgin olive oil
Handful of flat-leaf parsley leaves, chopped
75g/3oz Stilton or a local blue cheese, sliced or crumbled
25g/1oz walnuts, coarsely chopped

Ingredients for 4

2 pears, peeled, cored and sliced
Little lemon juice
50g/2oz watercress or rocket leaves
3 tomatoes, seeded and chopped
2 tbsp sherry vinegar
4 tbsp extra virgin olive oil
Handful flat-leaf parsley leaves, chopped
175g/6oz Stilton or a local blue cheese, sliced or crumbled
50g/2oz walnuts, coarsely chopped

1 Toss the pear in the lemon juice and arrange on four individual plates. Divide the leaves into four and pile on top of the pear.

2 Place the tomato in a bowl and toss with the vinegar, oil and parsley. Season with a little pepper.

3 Arrange the cheese and nuts on the plate and spoon over the tomato mixture.

snacks
treats^{and}

Herby Scrambled Eggs

Quick and Easy

Farmer's markets are a great place to get your free-range or organic eggs, which are often cheaper than in the shops. You can also talk to your supplier to find out if they truly are free-range eggs. Sadly, there is a big difference in the degree of free range allowed and some chickens are not as free as the label may suggest.

Ingredients for 2

4 free-range eggs
3 tbsp milk or cream
15g/½oz butter
3 tbsp soft-leaf fresh herbs
    e.g. parsley, basil,
chervil, sage, chopped
40g/1½oz hard cheese,
    grated
Salt and freshly ground
    black pepper
Buttered toast to serve

Ingredients for 4

8 free-range eggs
6 tbsp milk or cream
25g/1oz butter
6 tbsp soft-leaf fresh herbs
    e.g. parsley, basil, chervil,
    sage, chopped
75g/3oz hard cheese, grated
Salt and freshly ground
    black pepper
Buttered toast to serve

1 Place the eggs in a mixing bowl with the milk and seasoning and whisk until well combined.

2 Heat the butter in a heavy-based saucepan or frying pan over a medium heat and pour in the eggs.

3 Using a wooden spoon or fork, stir the egg mixture continuously as it cooks. Continue to cook until most, but not all of the egg has set.

4 Remove from the heat and stir in the herbs and cheese. Continue to stir for a further minute or two as the eggs continue to cook in the residue heat of the pan.

5 Serve on buttered toast.

Quails' Eggs with Tarragon Mayonnaise

Easy Entertaining

This makes an elegant starter or light supper dish. The mayonnaise will keep in the refrigerator for up to one week. The rapeseed oil has a mild flavour and will give a strong yellow colour. Groundnut oil also has a mild flavour, but will give a paler mayonnaise.

Mayonnaise:

1 free-range egg
½ tsp mustard powder
2 tsp tarragon vinegar
200ml/7fl oz extra virgin rapeseed or groundnut oil
1 tsp chopped fresh tarragon
Salt and white pepper

Ingredients for 2

6 free-range quails' eggs
25g/1oz rocket, watercress or
    mixed green salad leaves
Brown bread to serve

Ingredients for 4

12 free-range quails' eggs
50g/2oz rocket, watercress
or mixed green salad leaves
Brown bread to serve

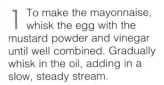

1 To make the mayonnaise, whisk the egg with the mustard powder and vinegar until well combined. Gradually whisk in the oil, adding in a slow, steady stream.

2 Stir in the tarragon and season with salt and pepper. Chill until required.

3 Bring a pan of water to the boil. Carefully lower in the eggs and boil for 3 minutes. Drain gently, tap the shells and run under cold water for a few minutes to cool.

4 To shell the eggs, roll the eggs on a board until the shell has cracked all over. Then carefully pull away the shell.

5 Pile the salad leaves onto plates and arrange eggs, whole or halved, on the plates.

6 Spoon over a little mayonnaise and serve the rest separately.

7 Serve with thin slices of brown bread.

Honey Mustard Dressing & Honey Mustard Glaze

Quick and Easy

I am lucky enough to have a supplier of both hand-made mustards and honey at my local farmer's market. Both of these two ingredients are popular flavours in my kitchen. Here, they are combined to form a versatile salad dressing and a great glaze for meat or poultry.

Honey Mustard Salad Dressing:

Ingredients for 2

1 tbsp clear honey
1 tbsp whole grain mustard
2 tbsp olive oil
1 tbsp white wine vinegar
Salt and freshly ground
 black pepper

Ingredients for 4

2 tbsp clear honey
2 tbsp whole grain mustard
4 tbsp olive oil
2 tbsp white wine vinegar
Salt and freshly ground
 black pepper

1 Mix all the ingredients together with a fork until well combined.

2 Pour over a green or mixed salad and toss to coat.

Honey Mustard Glaze:

Ingredients for 2

1 tbsp clear honey
1–2 tsp wholegrain mustard
1 tsp olive oil

Ingredients for 4

2 tbsp clear honey
1 tbsp wholegrain mustard
2 tsp olive oil

1 Mix all the ingredients together with a fork until well combined.

2 Use to glaze pork, lamb chops or chicken portions before grilling or baking.

Gooseberry & Elderflower Fool

Easy Entertaining

Some farmer's markets have stalls selling fruit cordials and wines. Elderflower cordial is one of my favourites. It can be used to add flavour to fruit salads, fools and of course, makes a delicious drink in its own right.

Ingredients for 2

250g/9oz gooseberries
25g/1oz golden caster sugar
2 tbsp water
2 tbsp elderflower cordial
150ml/¼ pint double cream
125g/4½oz Greek-style or
    wholemilk natural yogurt

Ingredients for 4

500g/1lb 2oz gooseberries
50g/2oz golden caster sugar
4 tbsp water
4 tbsp elderflower cordial
300ml/½ pint double cream
250g/9oz Greek-style or
    wholemilk natural yogurt

1 Snip the flower and stalk ends off the gooseberries with scissors and wash. Place the gooseberries, sugar and water in a small saucepan and cook gently for 10–15 minutes until the gooseberries are tender.

2 Allow to cool and push through a nylon sieve. Allow to cool.

3 Stir the elderflower cordial into the gooseberry purée.

4 Whip the cream until standing in soft peaks. Fold in the yogurt until combined.

5 Gently fold in the fruit purée and spoon into individual dishes. Chill before serving.

Jam Tarts

Family Favourite

Little tarts made with an almond-flavoured pastry and filled with home-made jams are a delight, much nicer than bought jam tarts which tend to be too sweet. If you do not have time to make your own jams and preserves, buying them from your farmer's market is the next best thing.

Ingredients for 12

100g/4oz plain flour
50g/2oz ground almonds
75g/3oz butter, cut into small cubes
1 free-range egg yolk
A little water to mix
A selection of home-made jams of your choice, you will need
approximately 100g/4oz of jam

1 Sift the flour into a mixing bowl and stir in the ground almonds.

2 Add the butter and rub in with your fingertips until the mixture resembles fine breadcrumbs.

3 Add the egg yolk and enough cold water to mix to a soft dough.

4 Roll out the pastry and use to line a 12-cup bun tray.

5 Spoon a little jam into each pastry case and chill for 20 minutes in the refrigerator.

6 Preheat the oven to 200°C/400°F/Gas mark 6. Cook the jam tarts at the top of the oven for 15–20 minutes until the pastry is crisp and golden.

Honey Cake

Freezer Friendly

The sponge of this cake is flavoured with honey and is topped with a delicious nut and honey topping. Although the ingredients remain the same, the flavour of the cake will vary according to the honey you use. So, if you are lucky enough to have a supplier of honey which offers you different varieties, you can experiment to see what flavour you like best. The cake can be frozen for up to 2 months. Defrost overnight at room temperature.

Ingredients serve 10–12

100g/4oz butter, softened
50g/2oz golden caster sugar
150g/5oz local honey
2 free-range eggs
225g/8oz self-raising flour
1 tsp baking powder
50g/2oz pistachio nuts, chopped
75g/3oz glacé cherries, halved (optional)

Topping:
75g/3oz pistachio nuts
3 tbsp honey
Knob of butter

1 Preheat the oven to 180°C/350°F/Gas mark 4. Grease and line a 900g/2lb loaf tin.

2 Beat together the butter and sugar until combined. Beat in the honey.

3 Beat in the eggs one at a time. Sift the flour and baking powder together and fold into the cake mixture along with the pistachio nuts and cherries (if using).

4 Spoon into the prepared tin and bake for 45 minutes, or until a skewer inserted into the middle comes out clean. Cool in a tin then transfer to a wire rack to cool.

5 Whilst the cake is still warm, place the remaining pistachio nuts in a saucepan with the honey and butter and heat gently, stirring until combined. Spread over the top of the cake.

6 Allow to cool completely before slicing to serve.

Hot & Spicy Cider

Easy Entertaining

Some fruit farmers have been forced to diversify. In order to survive, some producers of apples have started to make apple juices and ciders. This is a lovely recipe, ideal for a good artisan-made cider. A slow cooker is ideal for keeping the cider warm when serving at parties.

Ingredients for 3

1 orange
25g/1oz golden caster sugar
75ml/2½fl oz water
600ml/1 pint dry cider
½ lemon, sliced
1 stick cinnamon
6 cloves
2.5cm/1 inch piece root ginger, peeled and sliced
Splash of apple brandy (optional)

Ingredients for 6

2 oranges
50g/2oz golden caster sugar
150ml/¼ pint water
1.2 litre/2 pint dry cider
1 lemon, sliced
2 sticks cinnamon
12 cloves
5cm/2 inch piece root ginger, peeled and sliced
Generous splash of apple brandy (optional)

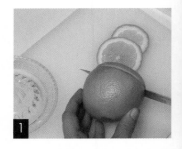

1 Slice half the oranges and squeeze the juice from the remainder.

2 Place the sugar, water and orange juice in a large saucepan and heat gently, stirring until the sugar dissolves.

3 Add all the remaining ingredients. Heat until just beginning to simmer, then reduce the heat and simmer very gently for at least 15 minutes. Do not allow to boil.

4 Serve hot in sturdy glasses.

Bruschetta with Cream Cheese and Roasted Tomatoes

Quick and Easy

A light lunch, starter or party snack, the choice is yours. Many farmer's markets have a stall selling breads. Here you will be able to find artisan-style breads in all shapes and sizes. It is a joy to try the different breads available, all so different from the often tasteless, airy breads you find in the supermarkets. Sourdough bread is a particular favourite of mine.

Ingredients for 2

**50g/2oz cherry tomatoes,
    use a mixture of red and
    yellow if available
2 slices sourdough bread
75g/3oz cream or curd
    cheese
A few fresh basil leaves
A little extra virgin olive oil
Salt and freshly ground
    black pepper**

Ingredients for 4

**100g/4oz cherry tomatoes,
    use a mixture of red and
    yellow if available
4 slices sourdough bread
150g/5oz cream or curd
    cheese
A few fresh basil leaves
A little extra virgin olive oil
Salt and freshly ground
    black pepper**

1 Preheat the oven to 180°C/350°F/Gas mark 4. Slice the bread.

2 Place the tomatoes on a baking sheet and roast in the middle of the oven for 10 minutes.

3 Brush the bread both sides with a little olive oil and place on another baking tray. Place in the oven above the tomatoes. Cook for a further 10 minutes until the bread is toasted and the tomatoes are soft.

4 Spread the toast with the cheese and top with the tomatoes and a few basil leaves.

5 Season with salt and pepper and drizzle with a little olive oil. Serve immediately.

index

Credits & Acknowledgements

A big thank you to my family, for giving up their time to accompany me on many weekend trips to farmer's markets. Their patience, whilst waiting for me when I was chatting to the stallholders, was greatly appreciated.

Thanks to all those who send their produce to farmer's markets, without whom this book would not have been possible. A special thanks to the stallholders of the farmer's markets at Barsham and Ellough in Suffolk and Blackheath, Marylebone, Peckham and Pimlico in London. Most of the food used for recipe-testing and food photography for this book was supplied unknowingly by them. Your produce is fantastic! Also thanks to those at the Borough Market at London Bridge, which, whilst not a farmer's market, is a fabulous food market nonetheless.

Thanks to Harrison Fisher and Co (www.premiercutlery.co.uk) for supplying the knives and some of the small kitchen utensils used for the step-by-step pictures. Thanks to Paul and Colin for their photography and also to Linda Salt who arranged for a fantastic selection of Denby (www.denby.co.uk) china and cookware which has been used in some of our photography. Also thanks to Magimix whose food processor remains a favourite bit of kit.

We would also like to thank The National Farmers' Retail and Markets Association for allowing us to use the images on pages 10, 13, 14, 18 left and 19.